HANDS ON!
33 *more* things every girl should know

HANDS ON!

33 *more* things every girl should know

SKILLS FOR LIVING
YOUR LIFE FROM
33 EXTRAORDINARY
WOMEN *edited by*
SUZANNE HARPER

CROWN PUBLISHERS, INC.
NEW YORK

Photographic acknowledgments
We have made every effort to trace the ownership of copyrighted material and to secure permission from copyright holders. In the event any question arises as to the use of any material, we will be pleased to make the necessary corrections in any future printings. Thanks are due to the following authors, publishers, publications, and agents for permission to use the material indicated: NASA: page 15. The Behle family: page 49. Rossmiller Photography, copyright © 1997, courtesy of the Behle family: page 51. Peter Da Silva, copyright © 2000, courtesy of Laura Scher: page 130. Bob Stanton, copyright © 1998, courtesy of HBO and Jessica Yu: page 161.

Acknowledgments for permission to reprint previously published material can be found on pages 171–172.

Published by Crown Publishers, a division of Random House, Inc., 1540 Broadway, New York, N.Y. 10036.

CROWN and colophon are trademarks of Random House, Inc.

www.randomhouse.com/teens

Book design by Elizabeth Van Itallie

Library of Congress Cataloging-in-Publication Data

Harper, Suzanne.

Hands on! : 33 more things every girl should know : skills for living your life from 33 extraordinary women / edited by Suzanne Harper.

p.   cm.

ISBN 0-517-80099-3 (lib. bdg.) — 0-517-80098-5 (trade pbk.)

1. Girls—Life skills guides—Juvenile literature. 2. Girls—Psychology—Juvenile literature. [1. Life skills.]

HQ777.H262   2001
646.7'083—dc21   00-045178

Printed in the United States of America

February 2001

10 9 8 7 6 5 4 3 2 1

First Edition

*"Be Prepared and You Won't Be Scared," by Colonel Eileen Collins as told to Suzanne Harper, is not copyrightable in the United States (17 U.S.C. §105). Any rights in this contribution which may be asserted outside the United States vest in the United States Government as author within the meaning of the United States Copyright Act.

DEDICATION

This book is for Audrey Kimble Harper,
Sierra Nichole Harper, Glenna Elaine Howell,
and Jessie Harper Pearson

ACKNOWLEDGMENTS

I'd like to thank Andrea Cascardi and Nancy Hinkel for
their help and good cheer throughout
the editing process; pediatrician Vicki Papadeas, M.D.;
my agent, Mitchell Waters (as always!);
and each of the 33 women who contributed their
eloquence, passion, and humor
to this book.

HANDS ON!

33 *more* things every girl should know

c o n t

ents

introd

Have you ever wanted to take a shortcut in life? Maybe figure out a way to get your homework done in half the time, or learn to ride a bike without falling off, or grow up faster without suffering awkward moments or making embarrassing mistakes?

That's perfectly natural. Everyone wishes they could skip some of the hard learning that life dishes out.

Well, the bad news is that there are a lot of lessons that you have to learn on your own.

The good news is that not everything has to be learned the hard way. After all, a lot of other savvy girls and women have traveled the path you're just starting out on. They've learned a few things along the way, and they've agreed to share in this book some of what they've discovered.

They'll offer inspiration by telling you how to persevere in spite of obstacles, how to live the life you want, how to follow your passions, how to become a leader, how to find balance, and how to do more in your life than you could possibly imagine.

They'll tell you how to nurture your relationships, whether those relationships are with your family, with your friends—or with yourself.

They'll also give you practical hints: what you should know about driving and fixing a car, how to whip up easy meals without a cookbook, how to save and invest money, how to become handy around the house, how to handle sticky situations with perfect manners, and how to swear off crazy diets for good.

If you don't find the answer to one of your burning questions in this book, they'll tell you how to find other trustworthy people to ask for advice. (They'll even let you know when you shouldn't listen to advice at all!)

The truth is, there's really no such thing as a shortcut in life; even the words of wisdom these contributors have to offer will still need to be tested—and lived—by you. Think of these essays as helpful signposts along the path of your life, sometimes keeping you on track and sometimes offering suggestions for fascinating detours.

Your journey is just beginning; I hope this book will help make it a trip full of excitement, daring, and—most of all—fun!

—SUZANNE HARPER

1

BE PREPARED
AND YOU WON'T BE

by Colonel Eileen Collins
as told to Suzanne Harper

Some people might look at the things I've done in my life—flying jets, para-sailing, and, of course, flying the space shuttle—and say that I'm a risk taker. I don't think of myself that way. I do things not for the thrill of it, but because I think they're important. Because of that, I've had a great career in the U.S. Air Force and traveled all over the world, and I became the first woman to command the space shuttle.

It's important to learn to take calculated risks in life so you can live your dreams, whatever they are. You can start practicing right now! Here's what I've learned about how to take risks:

1. DEVELOP A SENSE OF ADVENTURE AND CURIOSITY. I considered myself an explorer as a girl. I knew I was different in that way; most other girls wanted to do things around home or school. The house where I grew up was on the edge of town near a forest, a creek, and some hills. I would go out with friends and look for animals, build forts, and find hills to sled down. I felt I was the first person to ever walk on that land! Now, as an adult, I enjoy traveling and learning when I go different places. I've always been an avid reader, which is another way to explore.

2. WHATEVER RISK YOU CHOOSE TO TAKE, GET EXCELLENT TRAINING. When I was in college, I became interested in joining the military because I wanted a disciplined way of life with a disciplined job and environment, but I also wanted to have exciting, challenging jobs that changed every few years.

I joined ROTC in college, so the military paid for my last two years in col-

SCARED

lege, then sent me off to join one of the first classes of women in Air Force pilot training. Flying opened up a whole new world for me. I was constantly called on to do more and be better, which I loved.

We were trained to be exact in everything we did. Pilots have to be accurate in acrobatics, landing, formation, everything! The Air Force is very safety conscious, so we learned everything about safety in the air, ground hazards, mechanical hazards, and what to do if we faced dangerous situations. We would go through every scenario: What do you do if an engine goes out? What do you do if two engines go out?

Because we were so focused on proper training, I was never afraid; in fact, I loved wearing the gear (a helmet, parachute, and oxygen mask), pulling G's, and doing acrobatics in the air. The only thing I feared was possibly not meeting the standards that were being set.

3. WORK WITH A GOOD TEAM. Flying the space shuttle, in my opinion, is very safe. I thoroughly understand how it operates. I know the people who work on it, including many of the technicians, flight controllers, and managers. I trust them and I understand what they do.

4. IF YOU TAKE A RISK AND FAIL, DON'T GIVE UP. You're going to make mistakes, and bad things are going to happen in your career. You might as well accept that right now. A big part of your success will depend on how you handle those events. I've had failures; I didn't pass every flight I took in pilot training. I did well overall, but pilots in training take hundreds of flights, and most fail at least one.

When you have a failure or you don't get the best grade, you want to be the kind of person who goes back and studies what went wrong and learns from the experience. Don't let it get you down to the point that you lose self-confidence and never take another risk! That's the beginning of failure.

5. BE WILLING TO LEAD. Leading a group of people is one of the biggest risks you can take because you have to accept responsibility and authority. You can prepare for this role, too. This way, you'll be ready when you're the one who's being asked to lead. Here's how:

▶ **LEARN** everything about what your team is doing. A good leader must have technical knowledge of the workings of the group. If you're going to run the show, with people working for you, you have to know what they're talking about when they come to you with a problem or to ask for advice.

▶ **LEARN** to communicate and to listen. A good leader also has compassion, or a "people" side. This means that you understand if someone on your team has a personal problem or concerns that need to be talked about.

▶ **LEARN** how to be fair. You can't have people thinking that someone on the team is getting a better deal than the others.

▶ **LEARN** how to set a good example. For instance, the space shuttle flight I commanded was only five days long, and I wanted to get the most out of it. I knew from experience that if you don't get started in the morning, you'll get behind, so I was up and working as soon as possible. At the end of the day, I also needed to set an example and let everyone know that it was time to go to bed and get some rest. We could have stayed up all night working, but I knew that wouldn't be best in the long run. So I gave everyone a fifteen-minute grace period and then turned the lights out so we could all get to sleep.

▶ **START NOW.** You can prepare to be a good leader right now, in your own school or community. My first leadership experiences were as a child. If I was the oldest in a neighborhood group, I'd direct the games. (If I was younger, I'd let someone else take over!) Once you find something you really enjoy and become good at it, you'll naturally move into leadership roles, perhaps in the Girl Scouts or on a sports team. The more experience you get, the easier leadership will be.

Life can be risky, but it doesn't have to be scary. In fact, if you work hard and prepare well, it can be a great adventure!

2

WHAT I LEARNED
in cooking school

by Sara Moulton

I have always loved to eat. I cooked a lot when I was growing up; my mom and I even threw dinner parties together. But I always knew I wanted a career, so I went to college. I had part-time jobs when I was in school, including cooking in a restaurant and for a family, but I was studying subjects like pre-med and medical illustration. Nothing I was studying seemed quite right, and my mom could see I was floundering. She wrote to Craig Claiborne and Julia Child and asked them what I should do to become a chef.

Their advice: go to cooking school.

It sounded right to me, but I didn't want to leave my college boyfriend. Still, I packed my bags and headed to the Culinary Institute of America, in Hyde Park, New York. At first, I was depressed because I missed my boyfriend so much.

But on the first day of class, the students were handed chef's knives and cookbooks instead of pencils and textbooks. I was in heaven. That was the beginning of the happiest two years of my life.

(And that boyfriend is now my husband, which probably wouldn't have happened if we hadn't had that break. So the first thing I learned is that following your own dream always ends well!)

Cooking school and later working as a chef weren't always heaven, of course. For one thing, the ratio of men to women in cooking school was six to one—and those men had an attitude! They would say that women can't be good chefs because they can't lift heavy pots, they can't stand the heat, or they can't take the pressure of working in a busy kitchen.

Of course, the men who said these things were totally wrong. If a woman can't lift a pot on her own, she just finds a buddy to help. Women who have children or run a household know that those tasks require supreme calm and organization; I don't think there's a harder or, at times, more stressful job than these.

In fact, when I became a chef, I discovered that when the kitchen is very busy and the pressure builds up, the women stay calm, but the men usually crack. If a customer sends back a rack of lamb because it's too rare, a male chef might throw a temper tantrum and deliberately burn the lamb. A female chef is more likely to simply fix the food and move on. So the second thing I learned is not to listen to men who want to tell me I can't do something.

The third thing I learned is that if I want something badly enough, I can get it if I work hard. I was twenty-five years old when I started cooking school, and most of the other students were eighteen. I didn't even know how to use a chef's knife when I started, so a lot of the other students made fun of me. But I just kept telling myself that I was a good student and that I would do well. I progressed quickly, and soon the same people who had made fun of me were coming to me for advice or for help studying for tests.

I graduated second in my class, just one-tenth of 1 percent away from graduating first. I wasn't really a grade hound, but that achievement meant so much to me. Last year, my school honored me by inducting me into their "wall of fame," and this year I'm giving the graduation speech!

Although I've always loved to cook, I've also learned more about why cooking is important and why everyone should be able to cook.

First, cooking pleases people! Ninety-nine out of a hundred people just love to eat; it's a happy thing. So cooking is a great way to give a gift to someone. If a friend comes over or a family member comes home after a horrible day, you can make their favorite snack and brighten their day.

Second, I've learned that cooking encourages you to try new foods, which is a good idea. After all, if you take a bite or two and hate the taste, you don't have to eat it. But if you don't try something new, you'll never know if you're missing out on a great taste sensation!

Third, I've learned the importance of dining, not just eating. When you sit down to a meal with your family or friends and you've taken the trouble to light candles and set the table with cloth napkins, you create an atmosphere that encourages connection.

We all race through every day. Sometimes you can live with people and never really talk to them. My family eats dinner together five nights a week because I want my children to know that their day is important to me and their father. Everyone gets a chance to talk about their day and the problems they may have faced. People need that time to wind down, come together, and feel centered again.

From a nutritional point of view, taking the time to dine also helps you eat better. After all, it's very hard to maintain a good diet when you're eating on the go.

Finally, I've learned some easy recipes through the years that are great for beginning cooks (I've taught these to my own daughter, who's turning into a whiz in the kitchen!). Once you've mastered these, you'll be able to whip up a snack for yourself or your friends without puzzling over a cookbook, which is a great feeling.

Try them for yourself, and soon you'll be ready for other fun cooking challenges!

fruit smoothie

You can make this with either fresh or frozen fruit. Depending on the texture you want, you'll choose different types of fruit, but some basic possibilities are berries, peaches, and bananas (which add a creamy texture).

• Fill the blender about a quarter full of fruit. Top the fruit with plain yogurt until it covers the fruit with about an inch of yogurt on top.

• Add sugar to taste (this recipe does need sugar, but you can try experimenting to see what amount tastes best to you).

• Also add a little milk to thin the mixture. (You can use orange juice instead of milk, but the milk helps you get necessary calcium.)

• Blend until the mixture is smooth, pour it in a glass, and drink. (If you're patient enough to use just a little liquid and then keep turning the blender off and jamming down the mixture with a spoon, you'll end up with something like sherbet.)

french toast

This recipe makes enough French toast for one person or maybe two.

• First, break 2 large eggs into a bowl.

• Add enough milk so that when you beat the eggs and milk together, the mixture is a light yellow color.

• Add a capful of vanilla extract (the real stuff, not the imitation!).

• Beat the mixture together.

• Slice French bread into pieces that are ½ inch to 1 inch thick.

• Soak the bread until it's soaked through.

• Heat a nonstick pan and melt 1 or 2 teaspoons of butter until it starts to foam.

• Put the soaked bread into the pan and cook on each side until lightly golden.

• As the bread is cooking, put ⅓ cup of real maple syrup into a pan, add ¼ cup of frozen or fresh berries, and heat over low heat.

Pour the warm syrup over the French toast and enjoy!

> "You'll be able to whip up a snack for yourself or your friends without puzzling over a cookbook, which is a great feeling."

cheesy eggs

Stand a red pepper on a cutting board and, using a serrated knife, cut out a quarter of it by taking the knife down one side. Cut that quarter into chunks.

- Grate ¼ cup of sharp cheddar cheese.

- Throw the pepper chunks into a nonstick pan with 2 teaspoons of olive oil.

- Break 2 eggs into a bowl and add 2 teaspoons of water (to help break the egg up) and a pinch of salt. Beat the eggs until smooth.

- When you can easily stick the knife into the peppers because they've cooked enough to be tender, add the egg mixture to the pan. (You can also add fresh herbs, like basil, if you want.)

- Cook on very low heat, stirring a lot. (If you cook eggs on high heat, they get tough and watery.)

- When the eggs are half set and half runny, add the grated cheddar cheese. Put the lid on the pan and let the eggs cook for a minute or two so the cheese melts.

3

AIM
TO BE YOUR
BEST

by Cheryl Richardson with
Liamarie Johnson

I am lucky to have one of the best jobs in the world! As a "life coach," I help people create lives that they love. I encourage them to take good care of themselves so they can focus their time and energy on what really matters.

Clients decide to work with me because they're ready to make big changes in their lives. They might want to change jobs, simplify their lives, or fulfill a secret dream like writing a book. Our coaching relationship is a partnership, and each week we meet by phone to discuss the actions they'll take to achieve their goals. It's the most fun I've ever had working!

Although I've been trained as a personal coach and received the appropriate certifications, my best education comes from the people I meet.

Sometimes they're older than I am, and sometimes they're much younger.

My niece Liamarie is a good example. She's twelve years old, and I'm always amazed at what I learn from her. I remember a day last fall when we spent an afternoon together talking about life in general. During our conversation, we decided to play a game where she could ask me any question she wanted and I would do my best to answer.

To say I was surprised at the kinds of questions she asked would be a major understatement. She didn't want to know about boys, money, or sex. Instead, she had much deeper questions—the kinds of questions I'm still asking myself.

This is a recap of a four-hour discussion with my niece Liamarie. Our conversation covered many areas—career, life, money, family, body image, and friends. Liamarie asked many questions, and I've chosen five that I thought might be most important to you. She's a very wise young woman, and I'm sure her wisdom will help you, too!

LJ When I think about a future career, I have many different interests. I might want to be a veterinarian, a doctor, and a teacher. When I'm older, will I have to choose one, and if so, how will I know which to choose and whether or not I'll be successful at it?

CR The world is full of endless possibilities. You're very lucky. There are so many more choices available to young women today than ever before. The best advice I have to offer is to explore all your interests. Don't let others pressure you into deciding on a career choice too soon. Give yourself permission to dream big.

Contrary to what you might be told by your parents or teachers, having lots of interests is a good thing. If I had it all to do over again, I would have taken much more time both during and after school to explore a variety of career choices. By the time I finished high school, at seventeen, I felt enormous internal and external pressure to make a decision about the kind of work I wanted to do very quickly. Now that I'm older, I realize how crazy it is to expect a young woman of eighteen or nineteen to make important decisions about her future. Most girls aren't ready.

You have a long life ahead of you. And, as recent statistics show, you'll most likely travel down many different career paths during your lifetime. You may decide to become a veterinarian and eventually switch to teaching. No matter what you choose to do, if you remember the following tips, there's a good chance you'll be successful at whatever you do.

Choose work you feel passionate about. Instead of making a career choice based solely on your skills and abilities, be sure to choose a career that excites and inspires you. Skill will allow you to get the job done; inspiration will carry you through the inevitable challenges and slumps.

Maybe you're not sure what your passion is. Maybe you're a little afraid that you don't have a passion. Believe me, if you keep searching, you'll find something you're passionate about. Here are a few ways to help discover your passion.

First, realize that you may have found your passion already but not recognized it yet. Ask yourself this question: What is the one thing (or several things) that you always find time to do, no matter how busy you are? If you love to write in your journal or read books, perhaps writing is your passion. If you spend every spare moment playing soccer or softball, maybe your passion is sports or coaching. If you can't wait to pore over the latest fashion magazine, perhaps your passion is fashion design. Maybe you watch every nature documentary you can find on television; that could mean that your passion is documentaries or the environment. If you love hats, you could be a milliner; if you love animals, you could be a veterinarian; if you love the night sky, you could be an astronomer—or a poet. There really are endless possibilities.

Commit to being the best. Once you've chosen a path, do whatever it takes to be the best. Not only will this make you successful at what you do, it will allow you more choices. Leaders who are at the top in their field have more control over their future. Choosing to be the best means a combination of getting a great education and learning to communicate well with people from all walks of life.

What can you do to make sure you're always doing your best? First, figure out what time of day you do your best work, then set aside that time to tackle difficult tasks. Second, write to-do lists for yourself and check off each task as you finish it.

And finally, don't set up unrealistic expectations—doing your best doesn't mean being perfect, it doesn't mean that you always have to succeed, and it doesn't mean that you have to do everything better than your friends or class-mates. Perhaps you can write in your journal each week about what you think you did well or when you know you tried your best. That will help you keep track of how you (and not others) are doing in your quest to do your best.

Always put relationships before results. Throughout your career, remember that it's people who matter most. Invest a good amount of time in learning to communicate effectively. Make the quality of your relationships with others—a boss, co-worker, or client—your top priority. If you put people before results, you are sure to succeed at whatever you do!

These suggestions may not mean as much to you now, but hang on to them—they'll make sense later on.

LJ **How can I learn to feel good about my body and the changes that take place as I grow up?**

CR I'm sure there are many women (including myself) who are still try-ing to figure this one out. Sad to say, we continue to live in a cul-ture that trains young girls and women to strive for an unachievable goal—perfection. You can find evidence of this in almost any catalog or magazine that contains airbrushed and computer-enhanced photographs. Too often these pictures set the standard in a young girl's mind for what she should look like. The problem is, real women don't look like this.

So what do you do? First, get educated. Find someone you can easily talk with about your body and the changes that are taking place. It's important that you feel safe enough with this person to be able to ask lots of questions. Learning to be comfortable in your body is important, and the right informa-tion will help you to feel okay with the changes that are happening. You might decide to talk with your mom, an older sister, an aunt, or even a guidance counselor at school. It would be great if you could find someone who feels good about her body, too, so you can learn to celebrate the process of becom-ing a woman together.

Next, create a new habit. Make it a point every day to identify one thing you love about yourself. It might be related to your body and how you look, or it might be related to who you are, what you know, or what you do. It's important to remember that you are more than your body. Although a healthy relationship with your body is a good thing, it's only one part of a whole, wonderful you. Be sure to celebrate all of who you are!

LJ How would you define a good friend, and how does that definition change as you get older?

CR Before I answer this question, I'd be curious to know how you would define a good friend at this time in your life.

LJ A friend is someone who is trustworthy. Someone you can depend on and who will stick up for you in any situation. A good friend is someone you can talk to about anything without worrying about what they'll think of you. And a good friend treats you with care.

CR Sounds good to me! I agree with your definition, and I'd like to add a few ideas of my own. A good friend is someone who makes you laugh, someone who's fun to be around. A true friend will care for your relationship by always telling the truth. Although friendships will go through rough periods, making the commitment to talk to each other about how you feel will ensure that your friendship grows stronger over time. With a strong connection, you'll find that your definition of a friend doesn't change, it just gets better.

LJ When you look back at the times when your parents said no to things you really wanted to do, what advice would you give about dealing with the power struggles and the feelings of frustration that happen?

CR This is a great question! There is a certain amount of struggling that will always go on between parents and kids. It comes with the territory. I can remember feeling so frustrated when I couldn't do some of the things my friends' parents let them do. My parents and I had many battles of will.

The years from eleven to fourteen are the time when we begin to rebel a bit as we try to find our own place in the world. It might be the perfect time for you to start a journal or diary.

Writing about how you feel during particularly difficult times will help you to build a strong inner self that will guide you later in life. There will be many times during this period when you will not be able to do what you want to do, and rather than throwing a tantrum or causing a fight, writing about your anger may be a much better choice.

It might also help to see some of these power struggles as an opportunity to begin learning about how to deal with adversity. There will be many, many times in your life when you won't be able to have what you want. Learning to use the power struggles with your parents as a way to practice patience and understanding will serve you well as you grow into adulthood.

Start taking more responsibility for your life. For example, make sure that you do your chores and handle your responsibilities at home without having to be asked or prodded. Taking your responsibilities more seriously will help show your parents that you are growing up and therefore better able to handle some of the situations that you'd like to experience.

Finally, the truth is that living by your parents' rules is difficult. You can't change them, but you can always change how you respond to any situation.

LJ How do I deal with the two sides of me that may struggle to want to try something but know I shouldn't do it, like smoking, drinking, or drugs?

CR We are all tempted to try new things, whether they're good for us or not. As kids, we're especially attracted to those things that we've been told to stay away from. Once again I strongly recommend that you find an adult you can talk to about these feelings.

Talk to an adult about your desire before you do anything. Ask them to give you more information about how these choices might affect your life. And ask them to help you figure out how to say no firmly to friends who might be pressuring you to try something you'd rather not do.

HERE ARE SOME OF MY SUGGESTIONS FOR SAYING NO:

- Act matter-of-fact, rather than offended, if someone makes you an offer you'd rather refuse. A simple "no, thanks" is often enough. If you protest too much, people may feel it's a challenge to get you to do something you don't want to do.

- If you feel you must offer an excuse for turning down drugs or a cigarette, you can offer a legitimate reason ("I'm in training for soccer" or "I'm allergic to cigarette smoke").

- If your friends insist on pressuring you, even after you've said you're not interested, then it might be best to leave. You can either be forthright and say that their pressure is making you uncomfortable and you'd like to leave, or you can pretend to have something else to do that you totally forgot about until that minute, or you can just leave—you don't owe anyone an explanation for getting out of a situation that you don't like.

Speaking from experience, even though you might be tempted to try smoking or drugs, don't. Do yourself a big favor and decide right now that in spite of any desire you may feel, you'll make a smart choice and stay away from those things that will harm you and your health.

I still remember my parents always reminding me to be a leader rather than a follower. Although I didn't take their message seriously then, later in life I came to realize that choosing to do the right thing in spite of what others do is an important way to stand out from the crowd. Leaders stand out. Good leaders succeed. Great leaders make a difference in the world. If you stand up to pressure and make the right choice, you'll be well on your way to becoming a great leader!

GET CAUGHT
READING!

by Patricia Schroeder

Young people always hear adults talking about their youth like it was the greatest time of their life, very trouble-free. Mainly that's because we remember only the good things as we get older. Believe me, no one got to adulthood without real times of agony. So if you feel there are bumps on the road to maturity, don't think there's something wrong with you.

One wonderful way to deal with all the issues and concerns of youth is to read books. Whoopi Goldberg, Rosie O'Donnell, Oprah Winfrey, Dolly Parton, and many other famous people are passionate readers today and say books were the key to their survival as teens.

Have you ever heard people say, "No man is an island"? I wish they would also say no woman is an island, but what they mean by that is that none of us are totally unique. We are all connected to each other in many different ways. Yet when we are young, we often feel alone and isolated, like an island with bridges to nowhere and no one.

Often, young women think no one else has ever felt the way they do. That bottles them up, and they don't want to talk to anyone about their fears and feelings, anticipating ridicule. But books provide a wonderful and *private* way to discover we are not alone. Books allow people to bare their souls, to share their deepest fears and experiences. Finding people who have pondered or experienced things similar to what you've wondered about or been through empowers you, helping you feel freer to speak to friends about your thoughts and unlock some of the loneliness. This is what Oprah, Whoopi, Rosie, and Dolly mean when they say they never would have made it if books had not been there as a way to open new worlds to them.

Not only do books help you deal with the rough spots, they can help you decide what you may wish to do with your life, figure out where you may wish to live, or deal with many other things you worry about.

When I was young, I wanted to be a ballerina. I was passionate about it. You're probably wondering why I ended up in the United States Congress instead! Well, I read a lot of books about ballerinas from my school library. After doing all that reading, I realized that my desire was founded on fantasy, not reality. I just saw beautiful floating outfits and lovely music, not the constant training and travel or the likelihood of being considered over the hill at a young age—so I changed my career path!

Reading pushes your imagination ahead at full speed. New universes, intimacies, experiences, feelings, and ideas all come flowing out when you open the cover of a book. You get to use your imagination fully. For example, Brazil was a country that fascinated me. I read every book I could find on the Amazon jungle. It was almost like being there. I loved to read about flying, history, and many other areas. So did Whoopi, Oprah, Dolly, Rosie, and others.

If you're looking for answers to the big questions about your life—what your career should be, how you should live, whether anyone has ever felt the way you do—try doing what many famous people did during their youth while looking for answers: read books. Or if you'd like to escape into another world— a different place on the planet, a different place in history, or a fantasy world of pure imagination—read books. You will be exposed to a variety of ideas and people you could never touch without books.

Get caught reading! You can't get caught doing anything better.

HONOR THE
MAKE-DO
MAMAS
IN YOUR LIFE

by Lorraine Johnson-Coleman

It's always a good idea to take a moment to reflect on all the wonderful women who touch our lives in very special ways. I remember one woman in particular who taught me a great deal about the legendary "make-do mamas." A make-do mama is an incredible woman who is able to take the little she has and make it do what she needs it to do. It didn't mean that these women had all that they needed; it just meant that they had all they were going to get, so they had to learn to make do.

Well, I needed someone to remind me that these make-do mamas have left me a legacy of strength and survival, and that because they were able to make it despite everything, I can make it today. Luckily, there was a very special friend who was able to teach me a very valuable lesson just by telling me her story. I would love to share it with you.

Her name was Hazella. She described herself as one of this country's last good country colored women. (She didn't know anything about being an African American, and I would never be so arrogant as to rewrite her reality.) When I met her, she was close to ninety years old, and she told me with much sorrow how she'd watched all of her friends depart this world, finally leaving her alone in it. The last one to go, she said, was her best friend, Sister Alma. It turned out that it would be up to her to make sure Sister Alma had a decent send-off, despite the pitiful efforts of some young kinfolks who dropped into her life just long enough to bury her.

But even after the burying, Sister Hazella would still have some heavy hurting to hit her. Not two days after the funeral, she walked by Sister Alma's house to kind of check up on things, and it was there that she saw it: all of Sister Alma's cherishables—the portrait pictures that held all of her memories, the jellies that she learned to can from her mama, and the ever-precious regal rags that used to swarm about her like the finest of royal robes—just lying there for a cheap buy in a two-bit yard sale. Well, there was no sense in trying to talk to young folks—she'd found that out when it came time for the funeral. There was only one thing she could do, so she did it.

She went down to the bank and took out all the money she had except the few dollars it took to keep the account open, then she marched back to the house, looked right in the face of those hardheaded young'uns, and threw every cent at 'em, all the while asking, "Is this enough to cover the cost of a life?"

Then she gathered up all of her things, carried them home, and put them all away—just the way Sister Alma would have—with a place for everything and everything in its place. Then she was so tired, so very tired, so she sat down in the rocking chair that she and Alma had made together using corn shucks for a seat and worn-out plow runners for rockers. Then she just had to ask, "Alma, do you think they'll remember us, the make-do mamas?" Of course, she didn't get any answer. Maybe there just isn't one. All I know is, if we ever allow ourselves to forget those wonderful women of yesteryear, we may not be able to reclaim them as easily as Hazella reclaimed those keepsakes.

> A mother, she explained, births and raises her own children, and a mama, well, she raises everybody's children.

My grandmother used to say that there is a big difference between a mother and a mama. A mother, she explained, births and raises her own children, and a mama, well, she raises everybody's children. In her honor, I have made myself a promise. I will celebrate women—every single one of them who stepped into my life and touched me in a very special way. Women who did even when they didn't have to. Sisters who helped me shoulder some mighty big loads. All of the warriors who laid the groundwork for who I am today. Mothers are a blessing, but mamas are a miracle. Lord have mercy, without them, where would I be? For that matter, where would any of us be?

Glory, how I love my ladies . . .
The aunties, the sisters, the grannies, and the nannies
The missuses, the mamas, the madams, and the mammies
The blood mother, the other mothers, and the ones we called ma'dear
All those ladies who lived in grace
With spitfire spirits and souls of sweet lace
Who could saunter down decent street, still swinging their hips
Dab a drop of Vaseline and shine their lips
And when they rouged their cheeks of sweet honey brown
They shimmered like a rainbow across a muddled ground
They never knew that they would make all the difference
In a cold cruel world
With their hot-combed locks and their paper-bag curls
But Lord bless 'em and keep 'em
Because without them, where would we be?

LISTEN TO YOUR BODY

by Laura Lippman

I was fourteen and unable to get into a size 14 when I went on my first diet. It's a vivid memory. I was in a dressing room at a local department store, struggling to fasten the zipper on a green gabardine skirt. I wasn't even sure what gabardine was—I'm still not sure—but that skirt seemed magical to me, an amulet that could bring me anything and everything I desired.

The only problem was, I couldn't fit into it. My mother said, as kindly as possible, "I think you need to lose weight." I promised I would, we bought the skirt, and eventually I fit into it. Strangely—or perhaps not so strangely—the gabardine skirt was never quite the charm I imagined it to be. Years passed before I wanted to wear that off shade of green again.

Dieting also failed me as a transformation. No matter what diet I tried—and I tried them all—I ended up gaining some of the weight back. Not all, but some. From the age of fourteen to the age of forty, I seesawed between sizes

10 and 12. It wasn't the sizes that bothered me, but the very motion of the seesaw—up and down, back and forth, perpetually out of control. I wanted off.

I began by realizing I didn't need to lose weight. Doctor after doctor had shown me charts that insisted I was at a healthy, normal weight for my height, even at my heaviest. My friends told me I looked fine. (Well, most of them.) But the one voice I needed most could not, for the longest time, make itself heard. It was my own body, whispering: "Just listen to me, and you'll be fine."

You see, the brain gets all the buzz, but the body is pretty smart in its own right. The problem is, the body is too polite. The body is the quiet girl in the front row, the one who always raises her hand, only to be shouted down by that rude boy in the back of the class—aka the brain. The brain thinks it knows everything. But the brain is excitable, vulnerable to all sorts of contradictory influences. The mouth waters for an ice cream sundae, while the eyes linger on the bony shape of a swimsuit model and the nose picks up the scent of a pizza parlor. How can you unscramble those signals?

The key is being able to separate true desire from wants created by external cues. Smells, magazine pictures, television commercials, even our own feelings can make us think we crave things we don't really want.

In order to tell the difference between the food you think you want and the food you really want, you must learn to tune in to the body's quieter frequency. If you let it, your body will tell you when it's had enough to eat, when it wants an apple instead of a cookie, or when you've pushed it too hard.

Here's an example. It's a glorious spring day and you have just had your favorite breakfast in the world. You are pleasantly full, and you decide to walk your dog, taking in the tender, grassy smells of the new season. The day is so pretty, it almost hurts in a way you don't quite understand.

Suddenly the fragrance of freshly baked chocolate chip cookies overwhelms everything else. It seems integral to the beauty of the day. The smell is coming from a bakery down the block. You see a thin, pretty girl from the grade above you coming out of the bakery with a big, greasy bag of just-from-the-oven cookies. She looks like a picture in a magazine—more specifically, like an advertisement in a magazine—and you suddenly find yourself dizzy with longing for . . . well, what exactly?

BRAIN (SHOUTING): We must have a cookie!

BODY (MURMURING): Well, you know, I'm pretty full. I just had my favorite breakfast.

BRAIN: Yes, but a cookie would make me so happy. Besides, I've been thinking we should go on a diet anyway. So we have to eat all the cookies and bad stuff we want today, because we're starting a diet tomorrow.

BODY: We don't need to lose any weight, and I don't want a cookie right now. I don't think you do, either. I think you're hungry for something else.

BRAIN: Hungry for what?

BODY: I don't know. Maybe you want to look like that girl. Maybe you think having a cookie is the only way to celebrate this pretty day. Just the way you think having potato chips is the only way to make yourself feel better on a rainy day.

BRAIN: No, I want a cookie. I'm sure I do.

BODY: Then let's make a deal: We'll keep walking, and if we're hungry later on and I decide a cookie is what we need, we'll come back and get one.

BRAIN: What kind of way is that to eat?

Of course, it is the only way to eat. Eat what you want, exactly when you want it, and you'll be amazed at how smart your body is about such things. Your body has no desire to overeat or eat only junk food. The body is supremely sensible.

For this to work, you first have to learn how to recognize hunger, that distinctly hollow feeling that comes from the stomach. A lot of us never feel this, so we never truly enjoy eating.

Once you've figured out that it's truly hunger that's making you want to eat—as opposed to emotion or fatigue or the weight of a bad day—you have to figure out *what* you want to eat. This is tricky. You may think you're always going to want a Twinkie. But once your body knows you're not going to deprive it of anything it really wants, it becomes much clearer about its desires. The vague signal for "something sweet" becomes a clarion call for a peach or a nectarine. (You'll also find that the body is thirstier than you ever dreamed—thirsty for good old-fashioned water.)

But when your body clearly states it wants a piece of chocolate, it's best to let it have a small piece. Depriving yourself of a small treat now can mean a binge later on, because you feel so frustrated.

Once you've learned to decode the "what," you need to listen to your body's clues about how much it wants. If it asks for a brownie, don't give it ten. Many of us overeat because we plan to give up all pleasurable foods for the rest of our lives, subsisting on nothing but carrots and water. But if we stop thinking of certain foods as forbidden, we are less likely to overindulge in them. Give yourself permission to have exactly what you want, and you'll find you don't want it so keenly. Remember what it's like to overeat, how unpleasant the sensation is, how bad you feel. Why would anyone court that bloated, stuffed feeling?

Now that you know how to listen to the voices in your head, what do you do about the voices outside—the well-meaning mothers, fathers, teachers, grand-parents, and neighbors who exhort you to clean your plate at every meal? (Do they still talk about the starving little children?) How do you balance your body's needs against the constant warnings not to waste food?

Here's my little motto, which I use on anyone who chides me for leaving food behind: "Unwanted food is as wasted in my stomach as it is on that plate." More wasted, actually, because leftovers can be put away and eaten later. What can your body do with extra food? How many minerals and vita-mins can it absorb at once? What can it do but store it as fat, the body's equivalent of Tupperware, and about as attractive?

Learning to eat what you want sounds easy, but it's actually terrifying. There are no rules, no calories to count, no portions to weigh, no fat grams to tabulate. There are no good foods or bad foods. There is no right and no wrong. And, in the end, there is no perfection. "I don't want to be a size 2," your body may whisper to you. "That's not natural for me." Ignoring your body's natural shape and size can lead to eating disorders.

Once you start listening to your body, you have to agree to listen to every-thing it says. For example, I recently told my body I wanted a flat stomach.

"Forget about it," my body said. "It ain't gonna happen. Every woman in your family, even the skinny ones, have stomachs that go out."

"How about a six-pack, then?" I said. "You know, those really defined abdominal muscles?"

"I don't think so. But if you keep running and lifting weights, I think you'll have some nice definition in your calves. As long as you don't overdo it. The left knee tells me you're pushing it on your speed work. You're forty-one now. You may never be able to run a sub-eight-minute mile."

I sighed. "If I can't have a flat stomach, can I have a piece of pie?"

"Do you really want a piece of pie?" my body countered. "Or are you just feeling sorry for yourself and looking for some cheap comfort?"

"I truly want a piece of pie."

"Then have it, by all means. In fact, I think we want apple pie, heated, with a little ice cream on top."

7

HIT THE ROAD— SAFELY

by Lucille Treganowan

One of the most exciting days in most teens' lives is the day they get their driver's license. (The only driving-related experience that beats this is getting your own car!)

By the time you get that license, your parents, teachers, and driver education instructor will have told you a million times that driving is a responsibility and a privilege—and they're absolutely right. You'll enjoy the freedom of the open road even more if you're prepared for emergencies that you may encounter along the way.

Even if you don't have your license yet, it's good to know some basics about how to handle car problems. After all, you may be along for the ride when your older cousin's car overheats, or one of your parents may be behind the wheel when a tire goes flat. Why not be prepared for the situation (and, incidentally, capable of dazzling those drivers with your know-how)?

Taking a beginning auto maintenance class at a local car repair shop or community college is a great way to learn, in detail, about fixing your car. In the meantime, here are a few basic tips for handling the most common car mishaps.

> "Never try to remove the radiator cap immediately after your car has overheated. This can cause a serious injury."

WHAT TO DO IF YOUR CAR OVERHEATS

If you see the red warning light on your dashboard go on, indicating that your engine is overheating, here's what you can do right away to keep the problem from getting worse:

• As you drive, roll down the windows and turn off the air conditioner, which puts more of a drag on the engine. If the red warning light is still on, then turn on the heater, no matter how hot it is outside. This allows coolant to circulate and actually cools the engine.

• Don't idle your engine when you're sitting in traffic. Instead, put the car in neutral and step lightly on the accelerator to increase the RPMs of the engine.

• If you see steam coming from under the hood, pull over immediately. Open the hood so air can circulate and dissipate the heat; wait at least twenty minutes for the engine to cool. *Never try to remove the radiator cap immediately after your car has overheated. This can cause a serious injury.* Once your car has cooled down, add coolant if needed, then continue driving to your destination (if it's close) or to a nearby repair shop.

WHAT TO DO IF YOUR ENGINE IS FLOODED

• Don't pump the gas pedal; that will only make matters worse.

• Wait three to five minutes to let the spark plugs dry out. Once you've given the gasoline time to evaporate, the engine should start.

• To help the engine along, try pushing the gas pedal to the floor and cranking the starter.

WHAT TO DO IF YOUR DOOR LOCK FREEZES

There's nothing worse on an icy winter morning than to find that you can't open your car door because the lock is frozen. Here are two tricks to try:

• Try unlocking one of the other doors on the car. It may be that the driver's door lock is frozen because of the direction of the wind, but other locks are fine.

• Hold the key directly over the flame of a cigarette lighter, match, or candle until it heats. Then stick it in the lock; the heat should help thaw the ice. You may have to do this more than once.

WHAT TO DO IF YOU LOCK YOUR KEYS IN THE CAR

First, don't get mad at yourself—that will only make a bad situation worse! Just be sure to take precautions so that this causes as little inconvenience as possible. Here are some ideas:

• Have a spare set of keys made. You can leave them at home or the office; then you'll just have to take a cab or bus to pick them up. Or keep a spare set in your purse, so if you lock one set in the car, you have another set on hand.

• Call your car dealer and ask them to make you a new key.

• Call the auto club and ask them to send an expert in unlocking doors.

WHAT TO DO IF YOU NEED BACKUP

Many car emergencies are too difficult to handle on your own. For that reason, it's good to know how to get help quickly and safely. I recommend having:

• An auto club membership card. Having this card means that a team of car experts is only a phone call away.

• A cell phone to call for help. Cell phone calls are expensive, so you may want to promise your parents that you'll use the phone only in emergencies. Of course, you should never talk on the cell phone and drive at the same time.

• A preprinted cardboard sign, which you can place in your rear window, asking passing motorists to call for help. If you're waiting for help from either the auto club or the police, lock all your doors and stay inside your car until the help arrives. *Never accept a ride from strangers, no matter how nice and sympathetic they look.*

Remember, as long as you're prepared and keep a cool head, you can handle minor mishaps and keep driving fun!

8

FOLLOW YOUR

by Suzanne Falter-Barns

When I was a kid, someone was always leaning over me saying, "And what are *you* going to be when you grow up, little girl?" This was a ridiculous question at the time, because all I really cared about was whether Barbie's handbag matched her fur-trimmed sweater, and where my next package of SweeTarts was coming from. Still, I had my ideas.

Maybe I'd grow up to be a famous novelist, or a Broadway singer, or a fabulous movie star. On the other hand, just being a lady in a mansion seemed like a pretty good job, too. But what did I actually say when asked this question? "I don't know, maybe be a teacher," I'd answer sweetly, hoping that would get me off the hook. I certainly wasn't going to tell anyone what my real dreams were. That would be way too embarrassing.

So here is the bad news, and the good news. Dreams can be very

DREAMS
especially if they're embarrassing

The very best dreams are embarrassing because they contain that critical little piece of us that we never want anyone to know about.

embarrassing. Yet, at the same time, they are incredibly important—possibly the most important thing in your life, after the people you love. The reason they are embarrassing is because they come from that secret little inside place where all the really personal pieces of you bubble and stew. This is the same place where you store your crushes, your silent vendettas, and your plans to own and wear a really sexy red dress someday. This is also the place that great songs and ideas come from, along with the tears you wish you could avoid crying. This is the melting pot of your soul, the source of all your power in life. This is you, in a nutshell.

I think the very best dreams are embarrassing because they contain that critical little piece of us that we never want anyone to know about. It's as if we think our dreams and ideas are just plain too weird for the rest of the world. Yet here is the critical secret: We think we know what the rest of the world thinks of us, but we don't. We haven't even got a clue. We think if we tell someone that we want to be a writer, or an astronaut, or a veterinarian, or a cover girl, they're going to collapse into gales of laughter. We think we'll be laughed straight off the planet. In fact, the world is more welcoming than we will ever know. Believe it or not, the rest of the world actually does want to hear what we have to offer.

And the good news does not stop here. My old acting teacher, Allen Schorr, used to say, "If you're feeling embarrassed, that's a very good sign." He meant that if you're feeling shy and tender about your work, the rest of us will probably be moved by it. The first time I ever got up on a stage and sang a song that I wrote (which was certainly the most embarrassing thing I had ever done in my life), I got an enormous round of applause. Needless to say, I was amazed. People applauded my courage, I suppose, but more than that, they applauded the song, because I had to dig deep into my secret inner place to write it and sing it. And that meant they had to dig into their secret inner places to listen to it. So suddenly everybody had the experience of being truly, wonderfully honest for a change, simply because I got up and expressed myself . . . my real self.

These are the moments we all crave in life. And, believe it or not, they happen simply because someone decides to put up with a little embarrassment and follow their dream. The great thing about all of this is that the more you risk that bit of shyness and begin to do the work of your dreams, the easier it becomes. Your embarrassment actually disappears, replaced by great feelings of confidence and the lovely security of going to sleep at night knowing you worked on your dream.

Your dream gathers steam, and you grow in turn, becoming bolder and braver, strengthened by all the lessons that it brings.

Instead of seeing your dream as this big, cumbersome thing you have to get out there and prove, think of it as a gift. Because that's what it is—a gift to yourself, and a gift for the rest of us. Furthermore, it's a gift that only you can give. So when someone asks you what you're going to be when you grow up, consider the gift. How would you like to help people out? What is the truth that you need to express? Most important, what small, precious piece of yourself are you willing to share with the world?

I'm sure I'm not the only one who is waiting patiently to find out.

by Maggie Behle

The slow snow catches, hardly falling, hardly
and down to the pillowcase falls
black as knights
light and waiting
making her embarrassed blood run faster.

Some lie sick but
my body moves,
looking tight as he cries out
"Number thirteen in the gate!"

I pound my fists, static runs through me
countdown arrives,
I press my knee to the gate
I smile and hear the "three, two, one,"
sing to this war "three, two, one,"
which lets me go
out with pulses of dry adrenaline.

I am a ski racer. As long as I can remember, I have been a ski racer. And as long as I can remember, I have had one leg.

People always ask me, "Is it hard to do that with one leg?" I'd like to say, "How would I know?" I'd like to ask, "Is it hard to do that with two legs?" I don't want to seem rude, but I really don't know if it is hard to carry groceries, or drive a car, or ride my bike, or ski with one leg. If you're looking for a story or essay about someone who has overcome a disability, this isn't the one. I just have a disability; I didn't overcome it. To me, it's like this: I have blond

ACT ON YOUR

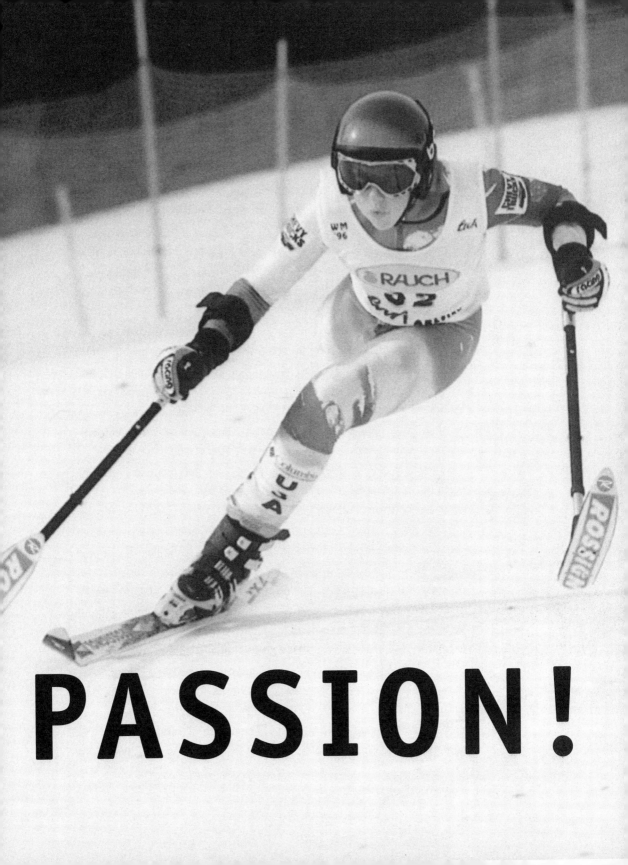

PASSION!

hair, you have red hair. I have one leg, you have two. I never noticed; I never thought things were harder for me, they were just done differently.

I grew up in Salt Lake City and was destined to become a ski racer. My mother took me skiing for the first time when I was four years old (she was a ski racer when she was younger). When my mom took my older brother skiing for his first time, she just held him between her legs and pointed him down the mountain. As you can imagine, this method isn't quite as effective for a one-legged four-year-old.

I hated my first day; it was cold, I fell too much, and I never wanted to go again—until the next time. The second time I went skiing, I took a lesson and learned with the proper equipment and a great teacher named Steve Peterson. After that, I wouldn't stop skiing.

At age eight, I started racing in Breckenridge, Colorado. My goal was to make the U.S. national team, so I trained after school and on weekends. At age fourteen, I made the U.S. Disabled Ski Team and began training full time for the Nagano Paralympics.

My first year on the team was hard. Training usually began at six-thirty in the morning. I was not used to this. I do not like to get up early. But as soon as I was on the hill, freezing in my downhill suit, going sixty miles an hour through a practice course, I was awake. After a while, getting up at five-thirty was worth it. I even looked forward to it! I loved skiing. I loved snow.

When I was fifteen, I went to Austria to the world championships and won two silver medals. I never thought I would be able to medal in a championship race, but during the races, I focused on having fun and going fast, and it paid off. Now I was determined to win an event at the Paralympics in Japan.

The next year, I won my first World Cup event in slalom. This only made me more determined to win in Nagano. I trained every chance I could get and went to as many races, disabled or able-bodied, that I could.

But in the spring season of 1997, I crashed in a downhill course and injured my ankle. A few months later, I had surgery and was in a wheelchair for two months. I lost most of my strength but not my determination. I worked hard and still was able to qualify for the 1998 Paralympic team.

My first race in Japan was a success; I came in third in the downhill. With my confidence up, I felt that would be my day to win in the giant slalom. After the first run, I was in second place, behind by only three-hundredths of a second. Now I knew I could win.

It was snowing lightly at the top of the hill when it was time for my second run. I was calm, I felt fine, I was ready. My first half of the course was the best I had ever raced. I felt great; I was going fast and being aggressive.

But on the flat, the easiest part of the course, my ski caught an edge and I fell. It was over. I sped down the hill past the television cameras, past my friends, and hid under the announcement booth. A friend handed me my Walkman. I put the headphones on and turned up the music as loud as I could. Three-hundredths of a second. A blink. An inch.

I looked out at the Japanese valley, fighting the water droplets in my eyes. But as I looked at the beautiful orchards and buildings, I realized that I had nothing to complain about. So I had never won an Olympic gold medal; so what? I was in the top five, sometimes the top three.

I loved ski racing, and this is what makes me love it: Survival. Challenge. Winning. Not winning. Some of my best days racing weren't the days I won, but the days when I felt like I kicked butt.

Now I live in California and study creative writing at Mills College. I live in my own apartment and am trying to learn how to surf and cook! I still love skiing, and I've started snowboarding. I'm learning to play the guitar and trying to write songs.

If you love life, it will love you back. My way of living was ski racing; now it's writing poetry. Yours might be becoming a tattoo artist or playing the bagpipes. Who knows? But know why it's your way of living—and act on it!

We climb this mountain
we sit on top
you have what I am missing
I have what you are missing
we forget
this is the way of living
this is the act of living
we see everything
we see nothing.

10

LEARN TO
SAVE
MONEY

AND
INVEST IT

by Neale S. Godfrey

When my daughter Kyle was four years old, I was president of The First Women's Bank. One day I was conducting a board of directors meeting and trying to act very serious and presidential. Suddenly, my secretary broke into the meeting with a panicked look on her face. "Kyle is on the phone and she says it's an emergency," she said.

Mothers all teach their kids to find us wherever we are if there is an emergency. Kyle was doing what she thought was right. However, our conversation went something like this:

"Mom, I'm glad I got you. I have an emergency!"

"Sweetheart, what happened?"

"I was watching TV and I saw a toy that I need and I want you to bring money home from your bank for me."

"What?" I screamed into the phone. All eyes around the board table were glued on me.

"Mom, I *need* money," Kyle whined.

My face was reddening, and I snapped back, "Where do you think money comes from?"

"Oh, Mom, it grows in the vault in your bank, and you go and pick it every day and bring it home."

My mouth dropped open. I was president of a bank, and my own daughter thought money grew in my vault! I had to get her off the phone, so I said, "When you grow up, you'll go to a bank and learn about money."

"But why isn't there a bank for kids? Why can't I learn about money now?"

Because of that conversation, I opened The First Children's Bank in New York. I also tried to find books about money for children so that my daughter could start to learn right away. Unfortunately, there were none. But, once again, she inspired me by saying, "So, Mommy, why don't you write money books for kids?"

I did.

Today, I have written thirteen books for parents and kids about money. (By the way, Kyle is now sixteen years old and very savvy about money. She wants me to tell you that, because she says this story makes her sound like a dumb kid.)

But why should you care about money? After all, you're young. Why should you care now if you grow up to be financially responsible?

You should care because over the next fifty years, $41 trillion will be passed on to you and your parents from your grandparents. Okay, not exactly *your* grandparents, but all the grandparents in the world will pass that wealth on to all the people in the next generation.

How much is that? Well, $1 trillion is $1,000 billion. Let's look at just $1 billion and try to think how much money *that* is. If you lined up one billion one-dollar bills end to end, guess how many times that line of dollar bills would circle the earth?

Give up?

Four times around the earth at the equator.

That's a lot of money to take care of.

It's also important to know about money so that you can make choices in life. When you grow up, you want to have a career that excites you and makes you want to leap out of bed every day to get to work. You want to have enough money to buy the things you want. Also, you'll want enough money to share some with people who aren't as lucky as you.

So, where do you start?

You start by earning money. You probably already get an allowance from your parents for doing chores around the house. (These chores should be over and above the chores that you do for free as a "citizen of the household." You're a member of your family; everyone should pitch in and help around the house without being paid. For instance, my kids have to keep their rooms free of breeding diseases as their "citizen of the household" chore, and they don't get paid for that.)

I suggest that you earn your age per week. So if you're twelve years old, you'd make $12 per week. Before you get too excited about your windfall, you should realize that part of the allowance system is learning to budget.

You can start your budget system by getting four clear plastic jars. Label them this way: charity, quick cash, medium-term savings, and long-term savings. Each week, on payday, you'll divide your money into the four jars as follows.

First, you'll put 10 percent of your allowance in the charity jar. You can work with your parents to select a charity you like. If you're interested in helping to feed starving children in foreign countries, for example, you could donate your charity jar money to UNICEF. Or maybe you're interested in helping the environment or saving whales or donating money to your church or synagogue. What matters is that you're sharing with others.

Next, divide the remaining money into thirds. A third of your money will go into the quick cash jar. You worked hard all week, so you should get to choose how you spend this money. Your parents have to decide the rules for quick cash. If they say no to candy or gum, then it's no—but beyond that, you get to choose what you want. Is there something you really, really want to buy? Then go for it! (If your parents try to steer you in a certain direction, just remind them that if you do make a bad choice, you'll learn from your mistakes. And ask them if they ever bought anything "stupid.")

The next third of your money goes into the medium-term savings jar. This helps you learn to push off instant gratification and save for something larger. Maybe you want to save for a CD player or a bike or Rollerblades. This is where you'll put the money for that purchase.

The remaining third of your money goes into the long-term savings jar. This jar helps you save for something even farther in the future and more expensive than what you want to buy with your medium-term savings—maybe your college tuition or a car.

At first, you should open a bank account with your parents and put your long-term savings there. The bank will pay you interest (money that you earn because the bank can use your money), and it's a safe place to keep your money. However, banks pay very low interest. If you want to earn more money with your savings, you should think about investing in the stock market (with your parents' help, since legally you have to be eighteen or twenty-one to buy stock).

This sounds more complicated than it really
is. Stock in a company represents ownership in
that company. So when you buy stock, you own a
piece of that company. People buy stock because
they believe that the company will use the money
in a smart way, so that the company's value will go up and the price of the
stock will rise, too.

The best way to invest is to do it on a regular basis. It's smart to buy stock
in individual companies you trust and know. Take a walk through a grocery
store with your parents and start reading the labels on the products you use
most of the time. Write down the companies that own the soft drinks, cleaning
products, or cereals you buy. Those companies could be good to buy stock in.

Another way to invest is to buy a mutual fund (which includes several
stocks) or a defined portfolio. A defined portfolio is like a mutual fund, but the
stocks are not bought and sold, but rather held. You can also check out a Web
site called Kidsenseonline.com, where you can find more information about
investing and take a money quiz to test your money smarts.

The most important thing to do is talk to your parents about money. You
need to understand how to handle money so you can learn to make wise
choices, and you need to start investing to build up your savings.

If you need help in convincing your parents that you should start a savings
plan, tell them this: If they had invested just $40 a week between the ages of
twenty-five and thirty-five and received a return of 10 percent a year, by the
time they were sixty-five years old, they would have saved $750,000. If you
learn to handle money now, not only will you be able to build a significant nest
egg for your future, but you'll also have developed an essential skill for leading
an independent, productive, and fun life.

Good luck!

11

REMEMBER,

Every Girl Should know
that even though she might have

thin hair she can't
do anything with...

or wild hair she
can't do anything with...

or eyebrows that
look like moustaches...

or zits...

or big ears...

or wear braces...

or bite her nails...

or be flat...

or too round...

or have thick ankles...

or bony knees...

or be shy around boys...

NOBODY'S PERFECT

by Ilene Beckerman

HI!!

She can still be...

YEAH!

☺

✿ A good friend...

A thoughtful daughter...

A caring sister...

A positive force in
the community!

♡ I love you

Thank you

BELIEVE ME, IT'S MORE IMPORTANT TO SPEND
YOUR TIME TRYING TO DO
GOOD THAN JUST TRYING TO LOOK GOOD!

gingy.

Bye now....

NOBODY'S PERFECT!

12

THE *rules* OF THE ROAD
WHEN IT COMES TO BOYS

by Norma Fox Mazer

I had a long talk with a young friend the other day about boys and life and school. Brittany is thirteen, she's her mother's only child, and she's in a struggle with her mother over how to conduct her life. Brittany wants to have a boyfriend and go on dates like other girls in her class, but her mom has laid down the law.

"She said no. No, no, no," Brittany reported. "She's like that, she won't say something just once, she has to say it three times. She says I should wait until I'm fifteen to date. Fifteen! I can't wait that long. My mother says everything starts too soon these days for girls. All she wants me to do is schoolwork. She's always after me to read. Read, read, read. Well, I don't like to read, it's not my major interest in life."

Brittany is pretty, with smooth skin the color of very light coffee and straight white teeth, courtesy of nature, not braces, and big dark eyes. When she gives me her shy smile, I can't imagine how boys could resist flocking around her. I asked her if she had a boyfriend now.

"No," she said, "I can't because of *her*. But there's this boy, Mitchell. We were friends, and then he got to like me." She looked down sadly.

"That wasn't good?" I said.

She shook her head. "Everything went wrong after that. He touched my butt one day. It made me mad," she said in her soft voice.

At first she was just steaming over it. Then she talked to a girlfriend, and they decided she should go to the principal and report the boy. He was called down to the office. She thought the principal or the counselor would just give him a big speech.

"No," Brittany said, "it was worse than that. He got three days in room fifty-three. We call it the iso room."

"The ice room," I said, alarmed. "What's that?" I had visions of the boy shivering in his underwear.

"It's a room where you get punished."

"What do they do to you?"

Brittany gave me a little sideways look that told me to cool it. I was getting too excited.

"It's a room where you do all your schoolwork, but apart from other kids," she explained. "Except for outside, you can't see or talk to anyone during the whole school day."

Tough, but at least it was isolation, not the ice torture.

I wondered how Mitchell felt after all that. "Was he mad at you?"

Brittany shook her head. "He came up to me and apologized. He said he was sorry he did that, and he knew it was wrong."

"Well, good for him," I said.

"Yeah," Brittany said, but she still seemed sad, thinking about it.

"What?" I said. "Don't you think that's good?"

"I do," she said without much conviction. "But now I feel sorry for him, because he had to be punished and it was my fault."

"Brittany!" I said. "It was not your fault."

> But now I feel sorry for him, because he had to be punished and it was my fault.

Sometimes Kristin cries and cries for no reason. I feel so sorry for her. I think Kristin just misses her mother too much.

"Yeah, it was," she said softly. "I got him in trouble."

"But he's the one who did something wrong. He touched your butt, and you knew that was wrong. You can't let boys touch your body just anytime they want to."

"I know, I know. I know all that."

"And so you did the right thing by not letting it go by."

"But we aren't friends anymore," she said. "When we see each other now, we just say hi and pass on. We don't talk to each other."

"Oh, I'm sorry," I said, but that seemed insufficient for losing a friend. And so while Brittany and I went on talking, I kept thinking about boys and touching and coming on to girls, and how a girl can keep a boy as a friend and still hold the line that she doesn't want crossed.

We got around to talking about Brittany's best friend, Kristin, who lost her mother three years ago to cancer. Kristin's father remarried about a year and a half ago, and it's really hard for Kristin, even though her stepmother, she says, is a nice person.

"Sometimes Kristin cries and cries for no reason," Brittany said. "I feel so sorry for her. Even though I get mad at my mother, she's there. I mean, I wouldn't want her to be gone, sick or dead or anything. I think Kristin just misses her mother too much, and no one notices or cares very much."

We took a break to make popcorn and peel apples to eat with it, and then we sat down again in my office. Brittany liked being in my office, which is tiny but really efficient, with everything within arm's reach. She said being in my office made her wish to have something like that for herself.

"So your mom is right," I said, getting in a little support for her mom. "You want something like this, you have to hit the books, study more, read more."

"Okay, maybe I will. Maybe," she said, bending over and letting her hair cover her face for a moment. "You want to talk about my friends some more?"

"Definitely," I said.

"Well, the thing about Kristin is that she doesn't let on to her parents how she really feels about stuff. In front of them, she's an angel. She has a sweet voice, she acts like everything is okay and she's the perfect kid. They don't know how she really is when she's not home."

Outside, it seems, something else entirely is going on with Kristin.

"She has a big, fat temper," Brittany said. "Whew! You don't want to get in her way. Not with me, though. She's nice to me, because I'm her best friend. But she gets mad so fast! You wouldn't believe it. She gets mad, and sometimes she hits guys."

Brittany repeated that last bit, just to make sure I understood. "She hits guys, and I don't mean a little old tap, like you give a friend. Norma, you want an example? She didn't like the way this boy, Sam, spoke to her, he was majorly fresh, made a bad comment about her butt being too flat. She went up to him and punched him in the face." Brittany made a fist. "Like this," she said. "She punched him. He had a big bruise on the side of his face."

"Where did she learn that?" I said. "Are they hitting in her home?"

"No, no." Brittany swung her head slowly from side to side. "Maybe she watches the guys, you know how they're always hitting each other. But it's different when a girl does it, isn't it? There's this other boy, too, that she slapped a thousand times—well, not that many, but a lot."

"Aren't you worried about her? I mean, if she was my friend or my daughter—"

"Yes! I just think sometime a boy is going to slap her back and really hurt her. I mean, they mostly have bigger muscles. It's funny, though, that she acts that way with some boys, but with others she doesn't even speak up for herself. There's a boy who likes her—"

"Who? You mean Sam, the one she punched?"

"Oh, no! This is someone else. Kevin. Kristin liked him, and it was cute that their names were Kevin and Kristin. We thought it was funny and sort of adorable, and it meant they should always be together. And they were, for like two weeks. But then she didn't like him, but he still liked her. He still does! He likes her, and he keeps following her. We could be sitting in the park talking about stuff, and we look around, and there he is, right across from us, sitting there, staring at Kristin."

"Does he say anything?"

"No. He just sits there like a squirrel. I told him to go away, but he ignored me. I told Kristin to tell him to go away. I thought he would listen to her. But she won't say anything to him about it. She says it makes her mad when he follows her, but . . ." Brittany fluttered her hands across her lips.

"Know what I think? She's sort of flattered, too."

"Smart of you," I said. "Feelings get really complicated sometimes, like the way you felt sorry for the boy who got punished."

"I know. I still do, but maybe not as much. I mean, I've been thinking— maybe I could have done it a different way, do you think so?"

"Yeah, I do. You could have talked to him, but still, it's good that he found out—"

"I know," she interrupted. "Don't get into a lecture. I get enough of those from Mom. Like, every other minute, she's telling me stuff. She doesn't know I'm good! I mean, I'm not boasting, but I'm not in trouble or anything. I have this other best friend, Julie. She might be going that way."

"What way? Trouble?"

"Uh-huh. She likes a different boy every week, which isn't so bad. She says that's just the way it happens to her, and I think that part is okay. Do you?" She didn't stop to find out if I did or didn't. "But the part that's not so good is that Julie doesn't go home. She stays out, from when school is over until suppertime. I mean, that's a long time. My mom doesn't let me do that. She's strict, too strict, but sometimes I can see the point. Like now, Julie's got this boyfriend, he's a senior in high school, he's eighteen, and he's going to join the navy as soon as he graduates."

"Wait. Whoa. Julie's your age, thirteen? And she's going out with a boy who's eighteen and they're spending the afternoons together?"

Brittany nodded. "She says he's mature and immature both. She says the immature part of him is fun, and that's what she likes."

"But what about the mature part?"

"She says she can handle it. But you know what? When I'm with Julie, I'm sort of like my mom is with me. I mean, I know how Julie feels. There was this older guy, not eighteen, but pretty old anyway, he was sixteen, and he stopped me one day downtown, and he said, 'Just had to tell you how pretty you are.' It was . . . it was . . . it was . . . I don't know!"

Brittany giggled suddenly. She had been so serious all the time we were talking, and now she just let loose with a cascade of giggles.

"So what happened?" I asked.

"Nothing! I mean, I talked to him for maybe four minutes, and then I had to go. I just said, 'Okay, bye,' and he called after me, all this stuff about remembering him when I grew up and stuff."

"I remember things like that happening to me," I said. "Older guys hitting on me."

"You do?" Brittany looked impressed. "Cool!"

"Yeah, but sort of scary, too," I said. "That's the way I remember it. Because they were so *much* older. You know, four years when you're thirteen is a big difference."

"Exactly!" Brittany said. "That's my point with Julie. I keep lecturing her, almost as bad as my mom, because she gets this look on her face when she talks about him. Like he's got her hypnotized. Sometimes she doesn't stay out with him, though, and she comes over to my house. I think that's much better, but my mother doesn't like it if she comes home from work and finds Julie there. She climbs the walls! She says that Julie is going to get into trouble, and she wants me to forget her. That's just so unfair, don't you agree? I can't desert Julie! What kind of friend would I be if I just blew her off? Anyway, all we do is talk about boys, we don't do anything wrong. I like boys, I like talking about boys, I like thinking about boys, I like *dreaming* about them! What's wrong with that?"

"In itself, nothing," I began.

"Hold the lecture," Brittany said.

I zipped my finger along my lips.

"Well, the other thing I was going to tell you, since we're talking about boys, which is my favorite topic in the world—did I say that?"

"Yes! About ten times, Brittany."

"Oh, that's just so you won't forget. When you get older, your memory's not so good, right?"

"I'm not having any problems remembering how you feel about boys, Brittany." I held out the popcorn bowl. "I'm stuffed."

"You can't eat as much, either, when you get older," she told me. "I'm not looking forward to it. So, what I was going to tell you about was my friend Rachel."

"Another best friend?"

"No, Kristin and Julie are my best friends. Rachel is a good friend. So

Uh-huh. She likes a different boy every week, which isn't so bad. She says that's just the way it happens to her, and I think that part is okay. Do you?

she's got these pimples and boys tease her, really, all the time, very mean. They call her 'pimple face' and 'pimple head.' They mock her so bad. Even the boy she likes mocks her, and she doesn't say anything, she just sort of smiles, as if she knows it's a joke. That's what he says. He says it's a joke and everybody should be able to take a joke."

"Humor that's mean isn't very good humor," I said. "Humor at the expense of another person—that's cheap."

"I totally agree," Brittany said.

At this point, her mother called to check in with her and find out when she was coming home. "Half an hour," Brittany said in a firm voice that reminded me of her mother. "Norma and I have a few things left to say." She hung up. "Okay, Norma, let's get started."

"What are we doing?"

"Making some rules about boys for my girlfriends. You know, like rules of the road for driving, so you don't get killed." She tore a piece of paper out of her notebook. "Go! I'm going to write this stuff down." She sat there, poised.

"Wait a second! I'm not Moses on the mountain. Let's do this together," I said.

And we did.

We decided that the first rule of the road was to be aware and honest. Honest with your friends and your family, but most of all with yourself. "Like, you don't kid yourself," Brittany said. "Like Julie with that guy who's too old for her."

"Exactly," I agreed. "That's such a big trap for everyone. You want some-thing, so you get dishonest with yourself."

"Like you know what's right, but you ignore it," Brittany said. "Okay. What's next?"

"Well . . . high on my list is being conscious of your emotions. Knowing what you are really feeling, not dismissing your feelings as silly or thinking that if you let them out, people won't like you. The more you recognize your feelings and respect them, the more respect you will get from other people. And that can mean speaking up. When a boy acts badly to you, you have to tell him. It doesn't mean being nasty. It's just explaining that this is how you feel."

"What if the boy doesn't get it?" Brittany said.

"Then you do the next thing. But you do the first thing first, which is to speak up for yourself. I know it's hard for people to do that, but if you say nothing about things that cause you unhappiness, it's as if you're agreeing to those things. Agreeing that it's okay to be treated that way."

"So do you think I should have done that with Mitchell, my friend—well, who used to be my friend?"

"Yes," I said. "And then if he didn't change his behavior, you do the next thing. Go to the principal or the counselor."

"Cool," Brittany said. "But another thing is, you should listen to your friends, because your friends, like me, will give you advice that's good for you."

"So right," I said, "because a friend who gives you advice is not emotionally involved. Take Julie and the eighteen-year-old guy. You know what's right for her, but she's getting all goofy and can't think straight."

Brittany was scribbling away. "One thing my mom says that I actually like is that every person deserves respect."

"Okay," I said, "that's the last rule of the road. Or maybe it's the first one. Respect. R-E-S-P-E-C-T."

"That's cool," Brittany said.

13

LOOK it UP!

by Barbara Wallraff

Most people own both casual clothes to wear around the house and fancier clothes for special occasions. In the same way, we also need to have more than one level of language stored up in our mental closets. There's informal English to use around the house when we're not doing anything special—to use in talking with our families and friends, however we want. Informal English may also be the right choice when we're writing stories or poems or song lyrics—when we want to share with other people what is going on in our heads, or in the heads of characters we have created.

The standard rules apply only loosely to informal English. Standard rules do exist, though, and what they apply to is called (guess what) standard English. I'm referring to a sort of dress code for words. Every girl—everyone—should know this dress code, these rules.

Why is that? Well, to begin with, for pretty much the same reason that everyone should know you're not supposed to wear a party dress to a softball game or a T-shirt and jeans to the prom. There's more to it, though. Clothes do say something about us, and they are like words in other ways as well—Samuel Johnson, who compiled one of the earliest dictionaries, once wrote, "Language is the dress of thought." But the main purpose of clothes is not to communicate for us or about us. Clothes keep us decent, and when it's cold, they keep us warm. Language, though, has no other purpose besides communication. And if we're all going to understand one another, we need to have a language in common.

Standard English is the level of language that the big American community shares. This is the kind of language spoken and written by the majority of the nation's newscasters and reporters, businesspeople, consultants, spokespeople—you name it. It's the language that earns respect, unless you happen to be working on one of those creative projects I mentioned earlier. Maybe you're a prizewinning novelist who writes in dialect, for instance. But even prizewinning novelists sometimes need to take a defective product back to the store and explain to the manager why they should get a refund. They sometimes want to write letters to their representatives in Congress about issues that matter to them. And when they do, you can bet they use standard English. This is the one level of language that we all need to have in our mental closets.

Now, although we don't usually discover new words by browsing in dictionaries—we see them and hear them in our lives—dictionaries are where we make new words ours. I don't know about you, but I love dictionaries. Not to keep on and on with this words-as-clothes analogy, but dictionaries are like boutiques or even department stores full of words, only everything is free. (I do spend money on dictionaries themselves, but anyone can use them in the library or online, and then thousands of new words are available for nothing.)

I am in the words business—an editor and language-advice columnist at the *Atlantic Monthly*. For many years I have helped professional writers solve their grammar, usage, and style problems, and lately I have been doing the same for the magazine's readers. You might think that by now I should have learned what's in the dictionary. But no—every day for my job I come across a new word or two, or wonder what certain words really mean, and look them up in one of my dictionaries. There are a lot of words in there: one big dictionary I have contains 450,000 words. Another one that I subscribe to online contains 750,000 words. Nobody has heard each one of these words—and of course no one knows what they all mean and is able to remember everything about them. Once, when I was talking with friends in a room where a dictionary happened to be sitting on a shelf, a couple of people began arguing about how to spell a word, as if this were something they could just decide. I wondered what was the matter with them. Look it up!

Then again, I was at a dinner party once and my host and I found that we disagreed about a word's meaning. Everyone else wondered what was the matter with us when we got up in the middle of the meal and wandered off to look the word up. I'm telling you all this so that you won't feel as if people who are good at language don't need to use dictionaries. People who are good at language are exactly who do use dictionaries.

Online dictionaries and ones on CD-ROM are especially convenient if you use a computer. Some of the newer ones have a little loudspeaker icon to go with each word; if you click on it, the program will pronounce aloud the word you've looked up. (I enjoy getting my CD-ROM dictionary to speak whole sentences to my cats: "You . . . don't . . . need . . . any . . . clothes.") Even printed dictionaries are more appealing than they used to be, with lots of drawings and photographs. (Do you know what a catfish looks like? How about a catboat?)

I'll admit that dictionaries are annoying if you don't know how to spell a word—you just have to keep guessing until you guess right, or nearly so. And if you're not using an electronic dictionary that pronounces the words for you, figuring out the pronunciation can be annoying, too—at least until you get used to the symbols that make up the pronunciation key.

Dictionaries can also be annoying if you're looking up a common word with dozens of meanings and you have to sift through them to find the one you want—or, even worse, to discover that the meaning you're looking for doesn't apply to your word. Persevere! At least lexicographers, or dictionary makers, tend to group related meanings together, so that you can skim until you get to the meanings that are more or less relevant, and then slow down and study the definitions more carefully.

A good dictionary will also tell you if the word isn't suitable at the standard level of language I have been talking about: It will be labeled "informal" or "slang" or even "offensive slang." And a really good dictionary will give you an idea of how to use the word in sentences, fill you in on its history, and let you know if there's anything special to keep in mind about how to use the word. It will do this job with a note, usually at the end of the entry.

For example, have you ever said something like "I brought the dress back to the store" and been corrected about that use of *bring*? If you didn't understand what the problem was, a good dictionary will explain it to you. (The usage note in the *American Heritage Dictionary* begins, "In most dialects of American English *bring* is used to denote motion toward the place of speaking or the place from which the action is regarded.")

Be aware that language keeps changing, and so if you're using an old dictionary, it may be unable to give you any clearer picture of current usage than your grandmother can give you about current fashion. For instance, the first edition of the *American Heritage Dictionary* published in 1969, noted that about two-thirds of the dictionary's usage panel refused to accept *contact* as a verb. That is, according to all those people, "Please contact him if you want a refund" was wrong. The latest edition, published in 2000, notes that about two-thirds of the usage panel did accept the verb this time around.

If you can figure out what to look up, a good dictionary can answer questions that are about much more than just what that one word means. Did you know that many people think that "She dresses badly" demonstrates good grammar but "She feels badly" does not? Look up *badly* and you'll see why. And then, once she is feeling better, are you supposed to say "She feels well" or "She feels good"? You should be able to find the answer by looking that up under *good* or *well* or both.

Because I like the dictionary to help me with questions like these, I believe in using the most persnickety, rules-filled, "prescriptive" dictionary I can find. I figure that I can always decide that I don't want to be quite as fussy as the third of the *American Heritage Dictionary*'s usage panel that still doesn't think *contact* ought to be used as a verb, but it's good at least to know that this bothers some people.

My favorite—as if you hadn't guessed—is the *American Heritage Dictionary*. To choose a dictionary for yourself, though, start by making a list of about half a dozen word questions that you would actually like to know the answer to.

Now go to a bookstore or the library, or search for the dictionaries that are online, and look your questions up in each dictionary you find. You'll get a sense of which one is easiest to use and which one contains the most information that you didn't already know—and let's hope the same one wins in each category! (If you come up with a tough question that the dictionary can't help with, ask your librarian about other, more specialized books such as dictionaries of synonyms and manuals of style and usage.)

Being able to track things down in the dictionary will give you not only knowledge but a measure of intellectual independence. Maybe you've already noticed that some people are only too happy to correct other people's language. But have you noticed yet that the people who do this are not always right?

I don't know whether I'm supposed to say this, but people often tell me that a teacher once told them something about language that nobody they've met since has ever agreed with. More often than you might think, what they were taught in school is wrong—or at least debatable.

Let's give their teachers the benefit of the doubt and say that possibly what the teacher told them was right, but they remembered it wrong. Sometimes they've been carrying wrong information around in their heads for years and years. (Why they didn't look it up a long time ago, and figure out the real story for themselves, is beyond me.)

When people tell you that you're saying something incorrectly, ask them why and keep asking until you understand what they mean. And if you don't follow it or if you're not sure you agree, look the point up in the dictionary later.

I remember someone once told me with great assurance that the phrase *whether or not* was always wrong. "There's no such thing as *whether or not*," she said haughtily.

Well! There's no note about that in any dictionary I own. It's true that most dictionaries don't have an entry for *whether or not*—but, for heaven's sake, each of those three words is in there separately. The attitude to take is that if a word or a phrase or a meaning sounds fairly normal and a good prescriptive dictionary doesn't come right out and object to it, you should at least keep an open mind until you've had a chance to find out more.

Is flipping through the dictionary as much fun as flipping through fashion catalogues? Well, okay, maybe not. But making a habit of using the dictionary will go a long way toward giving you a good command of standard English. And standard English in turn will give you a rich, varied mental wardrobe that will stay current for your whole life.

14

STAY CONNECTED WITH YOUR FAMILY

by Vanessa Atler

If I've learned anything over the last couple of years of my life, it would be how important my family is to me. When I first started gymnastics, I never knew that they would become such a vital support system. In his or her own unique way, each member of my family helped or inspired me to become the person and athlete I am today. They are all links to my success, and if one is broken, I will struggle.

My dad, I have such admiration for him. He's a very simple man. He loves my brother, Teddy, and me so much. He's not the best at expressing himself at times, but his love shows through in quiet ways. He seems to enjoy telling us jokes that aren't that funny. Somehow they still make us laugh.

He also gives us words of wisdom from time to time. When I've been stressed out during my competitive season, he will say something that simplifies things for me. I remember a particular hard time I was having

and he just told me, "Let the river flow, Vanessa." Such a simple statement, but at the time it seemed to make enough sense for me to let go of my tension. My dad is noble and painfully honest, and has a good heart. He kept me grounded when at times I was so far off the ground. I love you, Dad, for showing me simplicity.

Now, my mom—well, she's the risk taker in the family. She's taught me not to be afraid of challenges. She's usually the life of the party, and you can never be bored around her. (You know that kind of mom, the ones you like being around but you still have some apprehension that they might do something embarrassing in front of your friends, such as laughing too loud!) My mom is the drive and intelligence of the family, and if she was missing, we'd all be sitting around watching TV and complaining about how bored we all are. I love you, Mom, for showing me how to take risks in life.

My brother, Teddy, created the competitive drive I have inside me. Growing up, we were always competing and fighting over everything. Since he's a year older than me, I had to think up ways to survive under my big brother. Teddy also taught me what it's like to have a passion for something. He eats, breathes, and sleeps baseball. When he was little, he'd take his baseball glove to bed, and put his nose into it and inhale like it had this magical smell. I remember him watching *Field of Dreams* and having tears in his eyes when Kevin Costner played catch with his father at the end of the movie. My brother would also play hours of catch with my dad out in the front yard. And don't even think of disturbing Teddy while there's an important baseball game on TV! You could get your head cut off. His passion consumes him completely. Often gymnastics has consumed me, and I've learned this passion from him. I love you, Teddy, for showing me passion.

My dogs have also been an important part of my life. In my family, our dogs are considered human. We've had two dogs, both of them golden retrievers. My current dog is named George, and he is a tyrant around the house. He once stole my dad's sourdough bread off the table. Later that night, we saw a a big dirt mound in the backyard where he had buried the loaf. I love George for showing me unconditional love.

Two years ago, I lost Nubby, our first golden retriever. I loved that dog very much, and after his death I wrote this poem in his memory:

I MISS YOU, NUBBY

The house is empty without you here,
So many reminders to bring out tears.
The dog hair on the rug where you once had shed,
Even traces of it where you lay on my bed.

Outside in the back, your old tennis ball,
Marks still there from leaning against the wall.
The dog food on the counter no one's bothered to touch.
Why did you go? I miss you so much.

The ride in the car was really hard, you know.
I wish it wasn't so hard to let you go.
Saying good-bye before they took you away . . .
I wish I could have said something to make it okay.

For thirteen years you've been a true friend.
You even let me kiss your nose at the very end.
I'm sorry I wasn't brave enough to go in the room,
I just wasn't ready to let go of you so soon.

My mom, dad, and Teddy, watching them say good-bye . . .
When Dad closed the door, you even made him cry.
Because you were special to all of us, you know.
I miss you, Nubby, it is so hard letting go.

Although losing Nubby was hard, he also taught me something: how to deal with a death.

Gymnastics has taught me many things about hard work and discipline, but I know that if I focused *only* on gymnastics, I would not become a well-rounded person. I'm very happy that I did realize that and that I'm able to see the unique qualities of every person in my family.

I know from talking to friends that everyone gets frustrated with their parents and siblings at times; that's just part of growing up, I guess. But I think it's important to realize that your family also grounds you. Sometimes you don't even realize how much strength and support you're getting from them because it's such a constant presence.

But if you stop and take a moment to think about everyone in your family and what you appreciate about them, it helps you see that they're the ones who have really helped you become the person you are—and the person you want to be.

15

GET A **MENTOR,**

by Tonya Bolden

You remember Odysseus, yes? That Greek overachiever, protector of Helen of Troy, creator and commander of the Trojan War, who later journeyed the Aegean and Mediterranean Seas braving strange creatures, including the Cyclops and Scylla and Charybdis. Odysseus's son, Telemachus, had reason to be proud of his father, and considering all the time that Odysseus spent away from home, Telemachus was also grateful to his father for not leaving him high and dry, without a map or a compass. While Odysseus was off on his adventures, his wise and learned friend (and advisor) was looking out for Telemachus. That man's name was Mentor. He was Telemachus's teacher, and more: He was a coach, a counselor, a friend.

Your mother or father may not be sailing the seas and confronting monsters, but that doesn't mean that you can't use a mentor (or two or three) to help you chart your course in life and move steadily toward your goals.

There are all sorts of things that a mentor can do for you. In subtle and obvious ways, a mentor is someone who will put you through your paces and encourage you to challenge yourself, as well as give you a pat on the back when you have done well (or at least given an endeavor your best shot). Very often, a mentor will be able to connect you with people who can help you refine and organize your plans. This may be an introduction to a potential employer for part-time, weekend, or summer work. Or maybe it's an introduction to an administrator or faculty member of a college you're eyeing whose insights on that college will help you decide if it is the right place for you. Or maybe it's just someone who will hear you out on a subject about which your mentor knows zilch.

Will a mentor give you money? It's possible. Don't get the idea that a

BE A **MENTOR**

mentor is Santa Claus or a fairy godmother. However, should you need financial assistance in some worthy venture, a mentor may be able to help you out. And I do speak from experience.

There's a young man, Divivian, whom I've long regarded as a "play" nephew (but of late he's told me that he counts me among his mentors). He's a bright young man who has his sights set on becoming a doctor. I've observed him since he was about twelve (he's a friend of my real nephew, Bobby) and have known about his excellent grades in junior high school and high school. I've known him to actually read books that I've given him, and I once "caught" him, at age fourteen, reading (with no prompting from me or a teacher) one of the works of that awesome intellect W. E. B. Du Bois. So when time came for Divivian to go to college, I had a natural impulse not only to counsel him on courses, but also to help with his tuition. (Notice I didn't treat him to Air Jordans or some other fad.)

My relationship with Divivian also bears witness to the way that one mentor can lead to another.

After his first year of college, I introduced Divivian to a doctor friend of mine, Mona. (It's never too early to meet people in your prospective career.) Divivian was shy about making the call, but I pushed and prodded until he did, assuring him that Mona would be very receptive to any musings and questions he might have about charting a course to medical school. And she was, because I had told her about his academic excellence and sterling character.

So, you see, all your mentors don't have to be in your field of interest. (My last study of anything related to doctoring was tenth-grade biology, and I have seen maybe two episodes of *ER*.)

By the way, you and a mentor don't have to have face time. Some of my most enduring mentors are long dead. What's more, we never even knew each

other. The writers Anton Chekhov, James Baldwin, and Toni Cade Bambara are three such people. Their literary legacies inspire me to keep striving to produce useful, quality work. Journalist and anti-lynching crusader Ida B. Wells and civil and human rights champion Eleanor Roosevelt are among my mentors when it comes to trying to do honorably by others.

Among my living mentors are people I simply stumbled upon as I walked my road. One such person is an acclaimed writer who lives in the Northwest. I first met him on the phone in the late 1980s, when I interviewed him for a short magazine piece. (Before I got the assignment, I had, I confess, never heard of him.) When the interview was over, we talked and talked about writing; he encouraged me to keep at trying to be a writer, and he bid me keep in touch—or maybe that was just my imagination. In any event, I found unobtrusive ways to keep him abreast of my progress (like sending him a copy of my first book). Face time? During the dozen or so years that we have known each other, we have seen each other once. This occurred when he had a reading in New York City in the early 1990s, a reading I knew about only because he notified me a few weeks in advance that if I was interested in attending, he'd put me down on his guest list.

After the reading, I pressed through the throng and managed to get close enough to him to mouse out, "Hi, I'm Tonya." He smiled and gave me a hug (I think). We had perhaps sixty seconds of pleasantries before he had to get on with signing books.

Over the years we've had about a dozen phone conversations. Our communication has greatly increased thanks to e-mail, but there are times when no missives pass between us for months. Still, I always feel that he's there for me: When I've had a writing identity crisis or needed advice on a career move, he has always responded promptly, giving me clear, sound, simple advice.

What makes this writer mentor me? What makes me mentor Divivian? What made my doctor friend, Mona, open to mentoring Divivian?

Mentors are not totally selfless people. They do what they do out of enlightened self-interest: They want to play a part in shaping a future that they will be able to abide. There's no better way to do that than by investing in the young people who one day will be running that future.

Although a mentor ought to influence and shape you, a mentor should not be a Svengali or a Dr. Frankenstein. Beware the person who pressures you to be just like him or her, who tries to run your life. The good mentor doesn't want you to be a clone, but rather wants you to maximize *your* potential. It is essential that a mentor "gets" you: that he or she sees and understands who you are at the core, and respects your individuality.

Your mentors may be closer at hand than you think. Maybe it's the teacher who always gets after you about not working up to your potential, or the librarian who recommends books to you. Maybe it's the second cousin or uncle who's often remarked how much you remind him of himself when he was young. Or it may be a mail carrier or store clerk. You never know when or where a mentor will find you. Not every mentor will be with you for a lifetime; sometimes superb mentoring can happen in the space of five minutes.

The other thing you should bear in mind before you go on a mentor quest is that in all likelihood you will end up becoming a mentor yourself. It's contagious. Years ago, my most assiduous mentor, literary agent Marie Brown, said something that threw me for a loop. I was thanking her for all that she had done for me, from believing in me when all I had was two small-time bylines to connecting me with people who could give me work. "How can I ever thank you?" I asked, thinking she might tell me the name of her favorite perfume or flower or restaurant. Instead, she simply said, "Just do likewise." *Yeah, right,* I thought then. *What do I have to offer?* Now I find myself doing likewise and enjoying it immensely.

There are many local organizations that have mentoring programs:
- Big Brothers/Big Sisters
- Boys Clubs/Girls Clubs, Inc.
- Communities in Schools
- YMCA/YWCA

Or you can check the Internet. National Mentoring Partnership has a Web site: www.mentoring.org

16

EXPLORE
all your options

by Nancy Evans

Someone older and wiser once told me that I could be several things in my life, not just one. It blew me away.

Up to that point, I was paralyzed trying to decide what I wanted to be when I grew up. That's because there were a lot of things I wanted to be. I wanted to be the first woman president of the United States (that was in third grade). I wanted to be a journalist (that was in high school). I wanted to be a college professor (that was in college). I wanted to be a magazine editor (that was in graduate school). But when people asked, "So, what do you want to be?" I thought I had to have a single answer. Nobody ever answered by saying, "I want to do this . . . and that . . . and then maybe something completely different."

So I figured I'd be a teacher. I went to graduate school after college, to get my doctorate in English literature. I loved literature and its power to change people's lives, so the idea of teaching it someday was appealing. But deep down, I wanted something else: to work for a big magazine in Manhattan. When I say "deep down," I mean I was embarrassed to admit something like that because it seemed so far beyond me. Who would hire me?

Even though I loved writing and editing, and in fact did a lot of both in high school and college and during the summers, I didn't have much confidence in myself. That's an understatement. I was simultaneously reading books on fear of success and fear of failure. I was just globally afraid!

Then, while I was reading all these fear books, an older and wiser person came into my life. He somehow got me to admit that I wanted to work on a magazine. He'd worked on some of the most famous magazines around. And he basically said, "Kid, I'm here to tell you that you've got what it takes to work on a magazine. Go for it."

Well, that was enough to get me to stay up all night in my little dorm room, creating the first résumé I'd ever done and writing an impassioned letter saying why I wanted to work at *Harper's* magazine, one of my favorites. And then, eyes closed, I actually mailed it. Weeks went by. Nothing. Then something great happened. I decided not to take no for an answer!

I wrote another letter telling them why they should hire me. Since I'm basically shy and since singing my own praises is about the hardest thing on earth for me to do, this was a bold move. But my fear was obliterated by my passion: This was the thing I most wanted to do. Six months later, they called and hired me. And I learned the power of passion, a lesson I've carried with me ever since.

So there I was, working at *Harper's*. It was exciting. But I couldn't stop thinking that I wanted to go off and live in Maine and be a writer. I liked editing other people's writing, but I wanted to do my own writing. And I didn't keep it a secret.

That's when an editor at *Harper's* took me for a walk and said, "Listen, God willing, you'll have a long life, so why don't you consider this? Be an editor for now. Later, if you still want to go and be a writer up in Maine, you can do that. And if you want to go be a teacher, you can do that later. You can probably do a whole lot of these things over the course of your life."

This was big news. Up to that point, I'd felt that all these things I wanted to do wouldn't be there if I didn't do them now.

But the editor knew better. He took my youthful (shortsighted) perspective and transformed it into a grown-up (long-term) perspective. I was twenty-three years old. That change of perspective changed my life.

It also helped me become less fearful. I realized that when one phase of your life ends—not necessarily by your choice—you may feel scared, you may feel sad, you may feel anxious. That's normal. But you have to have faith and believe that something great is going to happen next.

And I learned that whatever I was most scared of was precisely the thing I most wanted to do. Hello, fear! Fear has led me to everything I've ever done in my life. Now I almost say out loud, "Okay, I'm afraid, and I'm going to do it anyway." Because here's the thing: The fear doesn't go away. No matter how successful you get, you'll still feel afraid sometimes. So say hello to the fear because it's telling you something important. The stuff you're afraid of is the stuff you want to do.

And then say what you really want to do out loud. Be brave enough to admit it. Practice saying it in front of the mirror (if that's what it takes!) until you can say it without nervously laughing or blushing. Because here's another thing: When you're able to tell others what you really want to do, doors will open.

Let me share that same thought, more eloquently put. It's from *The Power of Myth,* by Joseph Campbell. This is a quote that has inspired me in the past, and inspires me still; I hope it might do the same for you.

> **If you do follow your bliss you put yourself on a kind of track that has been there all the time waiting for you, and the life that you ought to be living is the one you are living. When you see that, you begin to meet people who are in the field of your bliss, and they open the doors for you. I say, follow your bliss and don't be afraid, and doors will open where you didn't know they were going to be.**

In large part because of that perspective, I now am grateful and appreciative of whatever I'm doing at any given moment. I don't have regrets about all the things I'm not doing, because I know their time will come. I am completely immersed in the joy of what I am doing right now. And I do feel joy; I have in everything I've done.

And just as the wiser and older editor counseled, I have done many things. After *Harper's,* I worked for several other magazines, some that were well known (such as *Glamour*); I even created one, *Family Life,* which is still published today. This happened because I had a dream of what a magazine for a mom like me might be, and I held on to that dream and never let go.

I also wrote for lots of magazines and wrote two books. I hosted a TV show. I ran two big companies and now have started another one with a friend, an Internet company for women called iVillage.com. I'm telling you this so you won't feel paralyzed by your choices. Make a choice and keep your other choices in your life plan notebook. Their time will come.

Maybe what worked for me will work for you. I'd try to see what I'd like to have happen—see it, visualize it, feel it, taste it, hear it. I'd listen to the little voices in my ear. Then I'd figure out the steps needed to make it happen, and write them down.

I kept it all to myself, of course. I was too scared to admit to anybody else what I wanted to do. But eventually I got braver and started writing it down and telling a friend about it. That worked even better.

It helps if you also do everything you can to move your dream along. Study as hard as you can. Grab opportunities to gain experience. Hold on to names of people you meet who can help you accomplish your goals, people who work in places you want to work or have done things you want to do. When I was younger, people would say, "Let me put you in touch with someone who can help you." But I used to think that was cheating. Fortunately, I got over it. If anyone offers you a lead, follow it. It may take you a step closer to making your dream happen.

Anybody can do it. And you can start anywhere: Improve your grades in school . . . read more . . . train to run faster than anyone in your class . . . learn to drive.

Pretty soon you'll get the hang of it. And believe me, there's real power in looking back and knowing you've made a lot of those dreams come true.

wear your personality ON YOUR SLEEVE

by Kennedy

If it were only so easy as dressing a salad to ready ourselves in the morning. For years I considered slathering myself in balsamic vinegar and bleu cheese, but opaque liquids can be so unflattering and clingy. And what a stench at high noon in early June . . . p.u. If one of my nightmares came true and I found myself having to go back to high school, I think I'd be better prepared in the clothing department. I would dress according to my own whims instead of getting caught in the accordion of other people's inhibition and insecurity.

Adolescence is the ultimate buffet, a time in your life never to be rivaled. Later on you might find the world a tighter box that demands square nails, beige suits, and a plastic smile. By the time you are confident enough to realize your fashion potential you might have some hack of a boss with baggy eyes and a sour puss demanding less color in your life and more wattage from your soul. So hurry up, start dressing like a spaz while you still can. Any fashion mistakes you make in your teen years will be lovingly recalled and even yearned

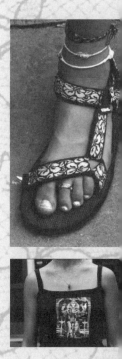

for the second you sell out to your first employer with a strict dress code.

I wish I had older sisters. I dressed like a guy the first two years of high school because I was afraid to offend anyone. I spent two good years in sweats and collegiate T-shirts. The pendulum eventually swung hard in the opposite

direction as I stole plenty from my mother's closet. I think that's where I developed a fetish for suits. I love me a good suit. The time I went to Paris the only French I used successfully was *"Acceptez-vous American Express?"* Talk about people-watching—a single day of ogling over the fashion sense of French women is life-changing. It is so important to find out what you like, I can't stress that enough. Everyone has some opinion and leans toward one way of dressing. It may seem impossible and costly, but you'll latch onto your true calling with a long and hard enough search. Not too many people outside the highest economic stratosphere can afford Prada and Dolce & Gabbana, so it is essential to look around in vintage and thrift shops for similar retro look-alikes of whatever you are going for and dive right in. Be careful. If you find at a young age you are attracted to handbags and shoes be forewarned that these fetishes turn into expensive obsessions and leave chocolate cravings and boy craziness dwarfed in their wake.

If you get daring and expressive enough you may go through as many as fifteen looks in one school year. It will be so much fun for you to look back and reminisce about your Goth period with the black lipstick, white pancake makeup, and sullen dourness, the hippie period with the patchouli oil, rafting trips, and Phish CDs, the punk rock girl phase with the global squatting tour, Sick of It All full back tattoo, and septum piercing. You'll marvel at your glamour phase, giggle at your skater fetish, and happily recall each phase as a part of a process that ultimately showed each bright side you possess and let you become who you are.

The truly interesting dressers are the fashion sharks, the ones who each season must create a whole new look for themselves or else die a miserable death. I was never one of these people. I get too comfortable in one pair of pants and, in between regular washings, wear them out over the course of a few months. The sharks are fun to watch because they are so self-conscious

and meticulous. The opposite are the fashion plaster casts who find one blah look early on and stick with it for fear of falling off some imaginary cliff if they stray too far. They never change it and become faceless with their predictability. I know a pretty girl from high school who refuses to bring any energy into her wardrobe because she's stuck in some ghastly late eighties time warp with the same bob, same liquid liner, same everything. She hasn't even gained weight! She never learned what she liked or what she disliked, as if any sort of flexibility in her personal style posed a huge threat.

I was almost irreparably wounded at an early age. When I was in second grade I decided to go out on somewhat of a limb with a demand for red satin disco pants. Oh, they were amazing, and what a complement to my roller-skating and rainbow headbands and Mork suspenders. I could have loved those pants, and, between washings, I could have lived in them. That is, until mean old Malinda came over, gathered a few of her friends in a circle around me, and started to laugh. Can you believe it? They are now, I can assure you, living a boring life of khaki and brown where a beige T-shirt from the Gap is a "crazy" purchase for them. I was demoralized, my young brow furrowed into a serious knot, tears creating dark red spots on my shiny disco frocks. Mom came to the rescue, bearing cords in hand, another fashion blow to the ego of the deprived. Oh well, I'm still hoping to bounce back and develop some more style.

People's words and thoughts are always daggers, no matter how hard you try to show them your tough shell. It is impossible to tell you to ignore what *everyone* else is thinking about you so you can tear through these years with color and glory dripping from every thread. Instead try and prioritize whose opinion is most important to you and reduce the number of people you are willing to compromise for. The ultimate

goal is to dress for yourself in things that you find attractive so each time you leave your house your clothes reflect who you are and what you see yourself as looking best in. Whether you are a shark, a Goth girl, or a prim and proper Pollyanna . . . wear your own style and live in your own clothes, between washings, of course.

18

How to Make an AFTER-YOUR-BOYFRIEND-DUMPS-YOU-FOR-YOUR-BEST-FRIEND Pineapple Upside-Down Cake*

by Tina Howe

1/2 cup super glue

1 cup earth

1 cup dog hair

8 slices canned pineapple

1 cup dust bunnies

1 teaspoon athlete's-foot powder

4 egg yolks

1 teaspoon saliva

1 cup Wite-Out

4 egg whites

1/4 cup rose petals

1. Bring super glue to a rolling boil in a cast-iron skillet. Try to stay calm as you ask yourself how he could have possibly left you for *her*.

2. Add earth and simmer five minutes, stirring constantly. Was he just *pretending* to like you so he could hang around *her*?

3. Remove mixture from stove and carefully fold in dog hair. Or was it the other way around?

4. Drain pineapple slices and arrange in the shape of a skull on the bottom of the skillet. Was she using you to hang around *him*?

5. Sift dust bunnies. Either way, the whole thing stinks!

6. Sift athlete's-foot powder. Boys are infants, but girls are mature, right?

7. Beat egg yolks in a separate bowl. *Right!* And what about Greg? She's been going steady with him for three years!

8. Add saliva and stir. *Three years!* Why would she be interested in someone else?

9. Pour Wite-Out in a separate bowl and set aside. Particularly *my* boyfriend. He obviously made the first move. The grass is always greener, blah, blah, blah . . .

10. Whip egg whites until stiff. Jerk! Lowlife! Loser!

11. Gently fold in Wite-Out. Poor Greg. He must be going crazy. . . .

12. Fold in yolk mixture, sifted dust bunnies, and athlete's-foot powder. He's no Tom Cruise, but he's a sweet guy.

13. Bake cake in a moderate oven (325 degrees) for half an hour. He has nice hands and a great smile.

14. Turn cake upside down and place on a platter. I should give him a call.

15. Let cool and garnish with rose petals. He could use a shoulder to cry on.

16. Serve immediately.

* Editor's note: This piece is meant as a joke and not as a real recipe. Do not attempt to follow the instructions, as either preparing or eating this "cake" could actually be harmful to you. The Publisher has to disclaim any liability which is incurred as a consequence of the use and application of the contents of this piece.

19

CELEBRATE A SABBATH

By Carol M. Perry, S.U.

"Hurray! Tomorrow's a day off!" We have all said this as we have seen national holidays and vacation periods on our calendars. But we need to remind ourselves that there were times in the history of the world when ordinary people never had a day off.

The wealthy people had slaves to do the work. These workers toiled day after day, with no breaks in their days and weeks and years, while the rich were free to watch others work and to enjoy their own leisure.

Of course, depending on the climate, the farmer of old had times of forced idleness, which brought little joy. In the cold northern lands, nothing could grow during the winter months, and the farmers worried. Would the days ever again get longer and warmer? Would the sun again coax the frozen ground to soften so the plow could prepare the acres for seed time? As the days got shorter, people were anxious that this process might not reverse but might continue until perpetual night overtook the day.

And so these pagan farmers tried to pacify whatever god was in charge of agriculture. When the harvest had been taken in, the farmer removed the wheels from his cart, decorated them with evergreens and candles, and brought them into his house as a way of saying thank you for all the work done and asking the god to wait with him and his family for spring to come. (The Advent wreath is part of that tradition.) Finally, as the days got longer and warmer, the time would come to put those wheels back for a new round of daily toil until the next harvest started the cycle again.

Meanwhile, in another part of the world, the Jewish people declared that one day in every seven was a day of rest and renewal. This was based on their belief that God had created the earth and everything on it. They wanted to celebrate this by taking time to appreciate it. They also remembered that they had once been slaves under a pharaoh in Egypt. Slaves had no holidays. The Jewish people could not forget that part of their history, but they could claim a day of freedom, a day to say, "I will not work today. I am no longer a slave."

The Jewish sabbath begins at sundown on Friday, with the lighting of the sabbath candles and a special family dinner. From that moment until sundown on Saturday, it is time to be a family, to rejoice, to pray in gratitude for both freedom and the good earth, and to relax. Jews try to not even think about work.

Wherever they have gone, the Jewish people have carried with them this important idea that for one day in seven, they should rest from work and renew their bodies and their souls.

Other religious groups have adapted this idea. Christians observe the first day of the week, Sunday, as their sabbath; Muslims keep Friday as a special nonworking day to acknowledge Allah.

When the first European settlers came to New England, these Puritans very strictly kept their Sunday observance, but they had lost the element of joy. Sunday was a day of no work, true, but it was divided between long prayer times in the icy little Puritan churches and a cold meal in homes where children were forbidden to laugh or play on Sunday.

The laws of the American colonies soon reinforced this idea. The early Dutch in what today is New York passed a law in 1656 forbidding a whole list of activities, such as sawing, hunting, fishing, dancing, card playing, bowling, and "ticktacking" (which probably was sailing), on Sunday. The next year, 1657, there is a record that the sheriff of Fort Orange, now Albany, arrested some men for playing *kolven* on Sunday. (This might have been an early form of golf.)

For many years, similar laws governed life in the United States. No business could be transacted on Sunday. Nonessential stores had to remain closed. Your grandparents might remember when one pharmacy in each town or neighborhood could be open for a few hours, as could a corner deli, but Sunday was basically a day of rest from buying and selling.

Since then, little by little, the laws have changed, and so have the people. Today, with so many different religious traditions, we would have difficulty asking the law to make sure we have a day to worship our God. However, we have lost something very precious.

There are still countries where the sabbath law is enforced, and it does make one think. On a recent trip to Jerusalem, I was interested to see a modern, bustling city change its face on Saturday. There was no public transportation. There were almost no cars on streets that had had monumental traffic jams the day before. The stores were closed, and so were the museums. Everywhere, families could be seen walking in the parks or having special meals. This day was treated as totally different from the other six.

Whatever your religious affiliation—or even if you have none—take a moment to consider what a sound idea lies behind taking time out. Everything around us urges us to do more, and the advertising world says, "Spend more." If the stores were closed, we would have to say, "Today I can't. This is my day to do something special." Maybe you could even say, "I am going to plan so that my homework is finished, since I want a special day to be a different person from a student."

In our world of computers and e-mail, of telephones and faxes, work seems to follow people wherever they go. One rarely has a chance to step aside, to do something different and so become a new person even for one-seventh of a week.

Psychologists tell us constant work isn't healthy. Our spirit needs some time off lest we become a modern kind of slave. If you are part of a religious tradition that respects one day in the week, be grateful for this practice that guides you to focus on something besides yourself. If you do not come from a religious family, it is wise to try to change your pace.

Think what you might do if either Saturday or Sunday were to be your sabbath day. And if it can't be the whole day, don't be afraid to start with an afternoon. That's not the time to clean your room. Get it done ahead of time. Try to do the same for your homework. Is there a book you've wanted to read, a park you'd like to explore, something special you'd like to do? Fill in that blank with one of those ideas you've been saving for when you have time. With a little planning, your sabbath time could become very special.

This can be your chance to say, "I am a free person. I am not trapped in a rut. I am enjoying a sabbath." You will have become part of one of the oldest and most special traditions in the history of the world.

20

GET MESSY

by Lieutenant Governor
Kathleen Kennedy Townsend

Skinned knees, muddy clothes, and tangled hair are a fundamental right of girlhood. Girls who spend all their time being neat and "ladylike" miss out on a lot of fun. Every girl should find something, or many things, she's passionate about, roll up her sleeves, and get messy.

Growing up, I was a pretty rough-and-tumble girl. My friends and I built our own secret clubhouse and spent hours in the woods seeking out adventure. My brothers and sisters and I waged touch football games that often left our clothes (and our lawn) a muddy shambles.

In fact, mud seems to have been a defining theme in my life. After I graduated from high school in 1969, I didn't know what I wanted to do with my life. Some friends of mine suggested that we work with Native American students, so we headed to a reservation in Arizona. In the morning, we taught English. On some afternoons, we planted pistachio trees in the hope that they would become a cash crop.

The bulk of my time, however, was spent making adobe bricks. Here's how you make adobe bricks: You mix together mud and horse manure. At first, my job was to stomp around in the mixture. Eventually, because I had such strong fingers, I was promoted to the position of squishing it through my fingers. We wanted to achieve the smoothest possible consistency: no lumps.

It was a great summer. The young people we worked with learned some English, and I learned a lot about adobe bricks. Perhaps too much. More important, I learned that I could make a palpable difference in the lives of others if I wasn't afraid of a little mud.

A few years later, I revisited the mud theme. In a college literature class, my friends and I read Mark Twain's *The Adventures of Tom Sawyer*. We believed that it wasn't enough to merely read and analyze the work; we wanted to live it. In order to understand Twain fully, we decided to build our own raft and spend a month floating down the muddy Mississippi River, just like Tom and Huck and Jim before us.

I had an additional motive for our journey that had nothing to do with southern literature. One of the friends I invited along was a graduate student named David Townsend. I had a crush on David, and I was determined that over the course of the month, I would show him that the two of us belonged together.

Many people doubted we could pull this off. Senator James O. Eastland, the senior senator from Mississippi, told my mother that it was a terrible idea and that he feared for our safety. He urged us to float down the White River instead. When my mother asked why, the senator responded, "Because it's in Arkansas."

Despite everyone's concerns, we met at a friend's house in Missouri that June and built our raft from scratch. We weren't very skilled, and it took us a lot longer than we'd thought it would. After ten days of grueling work, we hammered in the last plank, pushed off from the banks, and floated down the Mississippi.

We had a wild journey. We endured sixty-mile-an-hour winds, mosquitoes that could burrow through several layers of clothing, a twice-broken motor, sopping wet sleeping bags, the threat of poisonous water moccasins, and lots and lots of mud. We also met a lot of kind people who helped us along our way, including William Faulkner's niece, Deane Faulkner. We saw for ourselves the magic and splendor of the river we had read so much about, and David and I spent lots of time getting to know each other.

Mud continued to play a major role later on. One summer, I traveled to Greece to work on an archaeological dig. My affinity for getting messy was a big help, but I didn't have the patience. The Greek word I learned best that summer was *shiga*—slow down!

You don't have to go to a different state or country to really get messy. If you're a passionate environmentalist, volunteer to help clean up local parks and streams. If you're an aspiring athlete, join your school's soccer team. If you're a budding archaeologist, dig around in your backyard and see what you can unearth. And remember, getting messy isn't just about coming home covered in mud. It's about losing yourself in the sheer joy and excitement of what you love to do.

You'll be surprised at what you can discover. After my summer on the reservation, I finally understood what my parents and uncles had been saying for years about service and sacrifice. That summer was one of the first steps on the road of my career in public service. And as for my summer on the Mississippi? David Townsend and I are celebrating our twenty-seventh wedding anniversary next November.

21

PLANT

by Cassandra Danz

I became a gardener when I was twelve years old. I wish I could say I became a gardener because I had a deep spiritual connection with nature, or that I had the urge to express my high artistic ability, but I can't. That connection developed later. My gardening mania may have had something to do with puberty. My emerging passion may have been translated into a passion for nature. I don't know. The real reason I became a gardener was to annoy the heck out of my parents.

Instead of doing homework, I read great English garden writers like Christopher Lloyd, Russell Page, Vita Sackville-West, and Gertrude Jekyll. Gertrude Jekyll was my idol. I wanted to have a garden just like hers. She had pink roses cascading over walls and garlands of vines draped around the windows of her Cotswold cottage. She had a one-hundred-foot-long, thirty-foot-wide border filled with flowers that went from pale, cool blues to pinks to apricots to yellows and reds, and back to cool colors again as you walked down the path. She had a spring garden by an old well that had crocuses, snowdrops, fritillarias, tulips, and daffodils. She even had a special garden that bloomed only in September, made of asters and gray-leaved plants—really gorgeous stuff. She had a great eye, a real talent, and a staff of seventeen gardeners. Let's face it, she was rich. Her family had lots of money.

But in spite of lack of moola, professional help, or personal experience, I dreamed of making a garden just as nice, right where I lived. That was the problem. As you may have guessed by now, I did not reside in some charming English village, but in deep suburbia on Long Island, New York.

There was not one yard in my neighborhood that even faintly resembled Gertrude Jekyll's. Yes, there were houses with patches of lawn—a few strug-

a garden!

gling shrubs planted on either side of the front door. (They were called foundation plantings because the shrubs were used to hide the cheap cement foundation of the tract houses.) The homeowners absolutely had to have these plantings because they feared that somebody would notice the cement. Why didn't they worry that somebody would notice the ugly shrubs? Placing those bushes right up against the house was a cruel horticultural mistake. They were mostly evergreens whose native habitats were northern woodlands. Piney woods have naturally acid soil, which evergreens prefer. Those cement foundations were full of lime, a chemical that is death to acid-loving plants! So the local homeowners, like my father, had to go to the hardware store to buy chemical acidifier and pour it over the little evergreens just to keep them alive, much less thriving. It was just as well that the little trees were stunted. Under more favorable conditions, those pines, spruces, and hemlocks would have grown to 150 feet tall, and their roots would have gone right through our house's cheap foundation and strangled my uncle Morty, who lived in the basement.

I didn't blame my father or our neighbors for lack of horticultural expertise. Most of the people who had bought those houses after World War II were originally apartment dwellers, and so were unfamiliar with gardening. My parents, for example, had moved from a three-bedroom flat in Brooklyn to a three-bedroom house with grass around it. Land was a foreign land to them, so to speak.

My mother looked with suspicion on nature in general and the floral world in particular. In the yard next door there was a maple tree whose branches overhung our driveway. In the fall, the tree was in all its glory, a brilliant golden leafy bower of light. My mother glared at this work of natural art as though the leaves were ten tons of litter about to descend on her.

"Look at that," she'd say. "Something else to clean up!"

She once gave me a houseplant in a pot and said, "Be careful, darling, there's dirt in there."

Naturally, whatever my parents did, I wanted to do the opposite. If they disliked nature, I loved it! To me, the empty lawns and green spaces were an opportunity to connect with a world that my parents knew nothing about.

Even better, gardening was something that my parents found objectionable and incomprehensible! What could be more attractive than that?

Without asking my father's permission, I dug out a four-by-four-foot area next to the backyard patio. I loved the smell of the fresh earth as I shook the soil out of the clumps of grass, claiming a circle in the middle of the lawn as "Gertrude Jekyll territory."

I planted some lily seeds that failed to come up. Undaunted, I planted sunflower seeds, which did pretty well. Inspired, I went to the local nursery and bought two rosebushes with my baby-sitting money. One was called Queen Elizabeth, named after the current queen of England, a shrub with beautiful pink blooms that reminded me of Gertrude Jekyll's roses. The other bush had huge yellow blossoms, each with a beautiful pink blush at the edges, and it was called Peace because it was the official rose of the United Nations.

I got my father's shovel out of the garage, dug two deep holes, and planted the roses according to package directions. The soil of Long Island is very sandy, so it was easy going. I loved digging! There were interesting things down there, like earthworms, grubs, old pottery shards, and pieces of smooth quartz. I even enjoyed the struggle, the physical effort of cutting through the sod, lifting and throwing the earth. I had always been a klutz at sports and dancing in school, but shoveling was something even I could do.

I mixed compost and peat moss in the hole, planted the roses deeply, and watered them well. To my great satisfaction and joy, they bloomed their heads off. I can't tell you how wonderful this was for my self-esteem. So what if I wasn't beautiful or popular or clever? I could make something grow! And best of all, my parents didn't approve of it.

My father yelled at me because he now had to mow around my rose garden instead of running the Toro up and down his formerly geometric rectangle of a lawn patch.

To my mother's annoyance, I removed the plastic flowers from her favorite vase and replaced them with my real roses. When they inevitably faded, I put in some wildflowers collected from an empty lot nearby. She really hated those.

"Aren't they beautiful?" I gushed over my arrangement of daisies, daylilies, buttercups, and grasses.

"Weeds!" my mother sniffed. (She shouldn't have been so upset. At least they were legal weeds.)

It has been many years since I made my first garden out of perverse rebellion. I went to school, grew up, worked as a comedian, married Walter, and even had a child of my own, but all my life I have always enjoyed the pleasure and beauty of gardening, and you can too.

It's easy to become a gardener. Plants make such good companions: They breathe, they bloom, they respond to care and love, and best of all, they never talk back. That's what I call a great friend.

Even a window box or a few houseplants can be considered a garden. Fill a window box with earth and plant it with marigold, herb, or lettuce seeds for a miniature salad garden. You can even eat the marigolds.

Even if you can't afford to buy plants, you can root avocado pits in water, then plant them in containers. They will grow into five-foot trees in any bright location. You can plant grapefruit and lemon pits directly into containers of earth and they will also grow into handsome trees. All plants need is regular watering and a little attention, and if they die, well, you can always get another grapefruit or avocado and try again.

When my husband, Walter, and I finally bought an old house about fifteen years ago, I made a lovely garden just like Gertrude Jekyll's, only smaller. I taught gardening, did a radio gardening show, and wrote garden books. I became known as Mrs. Greenthumbs, and now even my parents are very proud of me.

22

ASK FOR ADVICE
when you need it

by Hilary Price

Have you ever felt anything made of lead? If you put a rock next to a piece of lead the same size as the rock, then try to lift them both, the piece of lead weighs much, much more. I couldn't tell you why (I'm no scientist), but it's interesting to me that something small can weigh so much.

I think secrets are the same way. Secrets (anything that you feel or think but are afraid to talk about) that you carry around weigh more than lead. They become this invisible thing you haul around wherever you go, and they can really wear you out.

The worst part about secrets is that they trick your brain into thinking that if you let one slip out, you'll be opening yourself up to embarrassment and laughter.

Worries work the same way. Between secrets and worries, we really make it hard for ourselves to relax and feel happy.

Here are some worries and secrets a lot of girls have as they grow up:

- **How do other people think I look?**
- **How do I talk to people I have crushes on?**
- **Am I fat?**
- **What if something violent happens in my school?**
- **How do I deal with kids flaunting their parents' money when I don't have that kind of money?**
- **What does it mean if my period's late but I haven't had sex?**
- **Will I ever like anyone who actually likes me back?**
- **What do I do if I don't "get" something in school that everyone else seems to understand?**

As I was growing up, I spent many hours alone in the bathroom examining my face in the mirror and asking myself questions like this. But one thing I never did was share these secrets. I didn't ask my parents, I rarely asked my friends, and it never occurred to me to ask an adult besides my parents. As a result, I had a lot of weight to carry around.

Now that I can look back on it, asking advice from an adult besides my parents about stuff that was bothering me is the one thing I wish I had known how to do. But first, let's straighten some stuff out about advice in general.

Here's one thing I've learned: Not all of it is good.

A lot of the time when you ask someone for advice, the advice they give you is what they would want to hear, and they aren't really thinking about what you want or need. This can mean that whatever fears or insecurities they are feeling will affect that advice, even if they are not your fears or insecurities. Here's an example. Your friend doesn't think you should date so-and-so, and tells you that person is a loser. But you find that person sweet. Is your friend really worried about you, or is she worried about what people might think of *her* if her friend dates someone out of the ordinary?

Chances are your friend won't even realize that it is her own insecurity, not your crush's personality, that makes her want to persuade you not to go on a date.

Here's another example for those of you who are the way I was and have never dated anyone. You want to go to a camp this summer, but some of your friends are going to stick around your hometown. You ask them if you should go, and they tell you camp is stupid.

Most likely, they are saying that because they will miss you if you go away, not because they really think camp is stupid. In situations like this, the bad advice isn't mean-spirited. It comes from their fear of losing your good company.

If you are trying to figure out whose advice is worth taking, ask yourself, "Is this person thinking about me and my situation or about them and their situation?"

To turn the tables, let's talk about what happens when someone asks you for advice. If you find yourself thinking about how their decision is going to affect your life, you aren't doing the person a scrap of good. (If your friend wants to go to camp but you don't want to be alone this summer, you're not in a good position to tell them whether or not they should go.) Sometimes the situation just feels too close not to think about how it affects you, and that's okay. But to be a good friend, tell them to go ask other people's opinion to balance things out.

So now that I've given advice a bad name, I still want to talk about why adults besides your parents (should we call them ABYPs for short?) can be good people to talk to.

For the record, it's not that parents are bad to talk to, but if you want information and don't want to get in trouble, these ABYPs might come in handy. I see ABYPs as anyone in, say, their late teens or older. They are probably a little removed from the daily storms of your life. They've been where you are and have managed to live through it. But who, exactly, am I talking about? Well, they could be your baby-sitter, cousin, soccer coach, or drama teacher. Maybe your neighbor, grandparent, rabbi, or youth group leader. A friend's older sister. Your mom's friend. Or even your mom's friend's older sister's baby-sitter (just kidding).

I could go on and start pulling names from the yellow pages, but the fact that there are plenty of people out there doesn't make it any easier to talk to them.

Believe me, I know. I never once asked an adult for advice about my personal life. As far as asking my parents, I think we had this unwritten code:

unless I got myself into some kind of big trouble, they didn't want to meddle in my life. (Which meant giving advice.) Since I didn't get into trouble, no advice was doled out. The upshot for me was that since they didn't give any, I felt uncomfortable asking for any. And for some dumb unknown reason, I extended this rule to all other adults.

I think this would have worked out fine if I hadn't hit puberty.

I hated puberty. I don't even like how the word sounds now, and it's been years since I actually went through it. It's not that I didn't know that changes were going to happen to me (I'd read the Judy Blume books); it was that I didn't want the changes. They all horrified me.

Here's a quick rundown of my "coming-of-age":

First, there was pubic hair. I tried shaving it off with my father's razor. To my dismay, it kept growing back. Then there was the whole bra episode, with my mother taking me to the store, picking out some bras, and passing them to me over the dressing room door. She offered to help, but there was no way I was letting her come inside so she could see me half naked. I was so uncomfortable with my new breasts that I could barely stand seeing them myself. Those "precious" years of young womanhood were spent in extra-large sweatshirts with my shoulders hunched over. Oh, then to top it all off, I got my period. My mother's heart-to-heart with me was this: "The pads are in the medicine closet in the hallway."

The worst part of it all was when I noticed one day that I had this milky white gunk in my underwear. I thought I had a sexually transmitted disease. I'd never even fooled around with anyone, but I convinced myself I had a disease anyway, and I got very freaked out about it. I didn't mention it to anyone—not my mom, not my friends. Can you imagine trying to bring it up at the dinner table? "Dad, could you please pass the salad? Thanks. Yup, school's fine. Yes, Mom, I promise I'll practice my violin tonight. I *know* my lesson's tomorrow and that I haven't practiced. That's because I've been obsessing about this white gook that dries crusty in my underwear. Got any explanation for me? What about you, Dad?"

My tactic at the time was to scour *Seventeen* magazine looking for any mention of it. This was pre-Internet, so I was at a considerable disadvantage as far as finding resource material on my own. It took *three stupid years* before I saw the words "vaginal mucus" in an article talking about normal vaginal health.

That I sat alone for so long in fear and ignorance makes me mad when I think about it, but what makes it even sadder is that it really never occurred to me that I could ask an adult besides my parents. Looking back on it, I see there are some things I could have done.

I could have used what I call the distancing tactic: Rather than asking my question directly, I could have asked the school nurse in more general terms if she had any books on puberty. She could have steered me to the book *Our Bodies, Ourselves,* which leaves no stone unturned as it goes through all the things that happen in a woman's body.

I could have taken the scholarly approach and said, "I'm doing a school report on _____. Can I ask you some questions?" (This way, I'd have gotten to ask my questions without exposing myself.)

I could have said, "Some of my friends and I were talking about _____ and they said _____. What do *you* think?" (Adults hate thinking you could be getting dumb information from your peers, and are likely to rush to correct it.)

There's the "I read somewhere that _____. Is that true?" approach. (No matter what crazy thing you're thinking—such as "Can you get AIDS from a toilet seat?"—you can blame it on an unknown author.)

And then there's the old standard: Start by saying, "I have a friend who _____" and then go on and talk about your worries like they belong to your friend.

Hey, I'm also all for taking a deep breath and asking the question outright. Except for the fact that when I was your age, I certainly wouldn't or couldn't have done that.

Lots of times, these ABYPs will pick up on the fact that you've got something on your mind, and they'll start asking you the questions. The pressure's off now. All you have to do is answer the questions, not ask them.

Okay, what if the person you asked doesn't pick up on the fact that you're disturbed about something? When asking advice from an adult, if you're not getting follow-up questions right away, it's probably a sign that they're not the right person to talk to right now and you should try someone else.

Never talking to anyone might seem less risky, but it's actually more dangerous. What happens is that big worries or secrets trick you into thinking that they've been written in permanent marker across your forehead and anyone who walks by can read them. Your problems start to feel *so* obvious to you that you think if anyone really cared, they would stop and ask you what was wrong.

If you get tricked into thinking this, you might try to play it cool, so you don't seem so pitiful in your own eyes. This is where the situation spirals downward. If you play it cool, you can't even hint to anyone that there's something bothering you. It makes it that much tougher to kick-start an adult into asking you questions.

But here's the thing about secrets: If something is worrying you that much, then that's the signal to reach out and ask an adult you trust.

Okay, the last hurdle is, who can you trust? When choosing an adult to talk to, sometimes you have to go with your gut to judge who is trustworthy. My aunt always talks about "the one brain cell that *knows*." I think she means that out of all the mixed feelings we have about a situation, there's a little part of us that recognizes the right thing to do.

The scene that comes to my mind is when I had just started college. I was at a bar, and an older guy kept buying me drinks. He said, "C'mon, it'll help you relax." But there was a part of me that knew he was hoping to make a move and thought he would have a better chance with me if I was a foolish drunk.

Even though I really wasn't attracted to him—and even though the little voice in my head had told me exactly what was going on—I did get drunk. He did make a move, and pushing him off me was like pulling a toilet plunger off my face. I made it home okay, but I wished I had followed my gut, which was telling me to say, "Go away."

Not every adult will give you good advice, but if you listen to the one brain cell that *knows,* you'll probably make a good choice in finding someone to talk to. And there are so many trustworthy adults who would jump at the chance to answer your questions. In some way, giving you advice lets us make up for the times we sat in our own isolation. And it makes us feel really good when we see that phew-I-asked-someone look in your eyes. We'd love it if you wanted to talk to us.

23

YOUR VOICE

is a ticket!

by Naomi Shihab Nye

VOICES

I will never taste cantaloupe
without tasting the summers
you peeled for me and placed
faceup on my china breakfast plate.

You wore tightly laced shoes
and smelled like the roses in your yard.
I buried my face in your
soft petaled cheek.

How could I know you carried
a deep well of tears?
I thought grandmas were as calm
as their stoves.

How could I know your voice
had been pushed down hard inside you
like a plug?

You stood back in a crowd.
But your garden flourished and answered
your hands. Sometimes I think of the land
you loved, gone to seed now,
gone to someone else's name,
and I want to walk among silent women
scattering light. Like a debt I owe
my grandma. To lift whatever cloud it is
made them believe speaking is for others.
As once we removed treasures from your
sock drawer and held them one by one,
ocean shell, Chinese button, against the sky.

When I was born in the 1950s, which suddenly seems a long time ago, many women still kept their thoughts to themselves, stood back behind men, nodded. I can remember my maternal grandmother saying "Never mind" a lot and disappearing into the kitchen. She wore an apron with clumps of quiet flowers on it. But she carried a wooden spoon like a spear.

I remember the mothers of friends huddled over their sewing machines in the evenings, answering their husbands in monosyllables, acting mousy.

Luckily, I also had women in my life who taught me that using my voice was one of the most important things I could learn to do. My mother had a stubborn, strong voice. She said white bread made people weak and pesticides were dangerous—and this was back in the days when few people talked about such things! We took vitamins and ate raw almonds. My mother insisted on buying our fruits and vegetables from an organic farm a few blocks from our house.

She dragged us there in a red wagon. Our laps were filled with small brown sacks by the time she pulled us home. The farmer still remembers her all these years later: "Your mother asked more questions than anybody. She was never afraid to ask questions. I saw that as a sign of healthy curiosity and high intelligence."

When I went to school, I had a second-grade teacher, Mrs. Harriett Lane, who urged everyone to memorize Emily Dickinson's poems before we even understood all the words in them, much less the concepts. She was an elderly, very stylish widow who refused to retire even though the school district was pressuring her to give up her classroom. She didn't see why she should quit, especially when she had so much experience.

On one of her arms, she wore multicolored plastic bangle bracelets, a fad of the time. She bopped us on our heads with them if we didn't listen. Despite our low-grade fear that we might get bopped, we responded strongly to her enthusiasm. Second grade was lively and fun. She honored us by never thinking anything was over our heads (except maybe her bracelets).

If we encountered words we didn't know, she said we should turn them over and over in our minds like lemon drops and get used to saying them. "Keep tasting words," she said, "and their meanings will grow on you."

Mrs. Lane taught us to recite poems and to sing in front of other people without shame. We stood on a stage, singing for one another. She urged us to use good posture, to believe in our dignity. We sang solos at PTA meetings. She said, "Don't ever apologize for your own voice! It is a gift that comes through you, and it will be your ticket, your magic wand, your tool to open all the doors."

To this day, I am never shy to say poems aloud or to sing in front of people, whether I know them or not. It feels as easy and normal as talking. In fact, sometimes it feels better than talking.

When I started writing my own poems, at age six, I felt enormous satisfaction to be able to go back to a page (a large piece of construction paper in those days) and find my voice still waiting for me there, in patient crooked lines. It almost felt like thinking twice. There was a comfort in it—you didn't lose track of so many thoughts and images. Also, I could change what I had written, which was comforting in itself. A voice on a page was different from a voice in the air, but both of them felt as precious as the glistening interiors of geodes cracked wide open.

I sent my poems to children's magazines from the age of seven on, never worrying about whether they would be published or not (considering the odds, I guessed one out of ten might catch an editor's eye) but feeling delighted when they were. The thought that a girl or boy living far away, in some exotic place like Bend, Oregon, or Providence, Rhode Island, might read my poem and understand it was thrilling. The written, published voice was a voice with wings—you could not predict where it might fly.

As I got older, new possibilities for sharing my voice presented themselves. The other side of the conversation felt wider and wider. As a teenager living in Jerusalem, I wrote the first teen column anyone could remember for the local English-language newspaper. Telling a bit about local goings-on, it was also a forum for musings, discussion of issues, recommendations of books, movies, and music, and so on. Of course, it helped that my father was the newspaper editor—some of my friends teased me about this. But I didn't care. I loved being able to write about all the names scratched into our ancient wooden school desks over the decades—the desks seemed to me to be collections of echoing voices. I wondered where all the people who had sat there before us were now. I loved to take up causes in print, creating a stir of dialogue and opinion. My own school asked me to leave after I publicly questioned some of their policies. This turned out okay—I liked my next school much better.

Back in the United States in high school, I worked with my friends on our school publications—the literary magazine, the newspaper. Our school was football-crazed in those years, having won a state championship some time before; it felt as if the literary types were operating in some secret margin of the universe. We had a miniature budget and didn't get much attention. But we determined to change that.

We dreamed up moneymaking schemes for our projects, knocking on doors throughout the neighborhood, collecting hand-me-down books for a gigantic book sale. We interviewed the cafeteria ladies while they were rolling enchiladas, presenting their voices and opinions with fanfare. We scheduled an all-school poetry reading, in which everyone who'd had a poem accepted for the magazine acted it out or read it, in costume, onstage, for all the English classes all day long. Decades later, people still come up to me on the street in my city and say, "I still remember that funny poetry reading you all did."

We put our voices out there in the air, where they could billow and jingle and connect like links in a chain. We weren't shy about being heard, and as a result, we felt our identities taking shape in the air around us. The football players weren't the only folks on earth. In fact, they started respecting us. I remember one of them buying me a mum when I was a senior, to honor the fact that I had never been to a football game in my life!

Later, in college, a teacher told us: If someone's voice touches you or moves you deeply—a play, a story, a novel, a poem—and the author is living, write to him or her. Share your response! It is important that you do this, so that voice will know it has been heard. It is your responsibility as a reader.

I was reading and loving the novels of the great British novelist Graham Greene at the time and wrote a huge paper about them.

Then I wrote him a letter, too, brazenly enclosing the paper!

To my surprise, he wrote back in longhand on blue air letter paper, something like, "I was having one of those days when I didn't believe much in anything I had ever written—then your letter came. How can I ever thank you enough?" Graham Greene thanking *me*? That was what using my simple voice did—put me in touch with the world.

Here is what I've learned—from my mother, from my second-grade teacher, from my college professor—about voices: Always know your voice is your essential, number-one treasure. Let it out. A voice hates being boxed up. It shrinks if you box it up. Don't be shy about speaking of the things that truly matter to you, even when no one else is mentioning them. Whenever you feel the urge to speak up, do it—whether it's in a classroom, in a group, on paper in a letter to the editor, or anywhere else.

Start talking and keep talking—remember, you are so lucky to live in an openmouthed time! These days students sometimes ask me if I am shy about sharing my poems since poems are "personal." I ask, "Aren't you personal, too? My personal part wants to connect with the personal part of you."

Celebrate the fact that the gender inequities of days gone by are mostly behind us. Girls now are raised to *know* they have as much to say (if not more—hey, face it!) as boys do. Anyone who doubts this isn't worth listening to. We know this is still not true in every country on earth, but thank goodness it is usually true in ours. Now and then we can still catch a shadow of a deferring woman over here—help shine light on it whenever you can. Encourage other people's voices, too. We should celebrate and champion the powers of the human voice every way we can.

Nourish and stretch your voice by reading and listening to other voices you admire, whenever you can. Read all kinds of literature and know you're never too old for children's books. Sometimes the clear voices in them will give you a compass when you need one.

If your voice embarrasses you sometimes, or doesn't always say *exactly* what you wish it had said, remember the same thing happens for everyone with a voice—actors, prime ministers, philosophers, athletes, poets, musicians, explorers, grocers. Now and then we all wish we could change something we said. Well, we can if we keep talking. Keeping a notebook in which you write at least three lines every day—about anything you see, think, wonder about—will help deepen your relationship with your written voice and other voices you

> Don't be shy about speaking of the things that truly matter to you, even when no one else is mentioning them.

" "

Anyway,
if you
never talk
to a
stranger,
how will
you ever
make a new
friend?

" "

admire. I recommend writing in it at the same time every day to get into the habit—right before you go to bed or right when you wake up is a good idea.

A popular piece of advice often transmitted to kids in the United States has been "Don't talk to strangers." There are even children's books centered around this theme. But I think it's crucial to keep it in context.

Obviously, you don't want to strike up a chat with a stranger in a dark parking lot at midnight. But what if you get lost somewhere—in an airport, for example? What if you need to know something in a library or in a store? So-called strangers are often just the ones able to help you. Anyway, if you never talk to a stranger, how will you ever make a new friend?

Of course, the most important times to use one's voice may be when it's hardest to: when you go against a group, when there are important issues no one else has mentioned. Sometimes people may resent you for using your voice; often that is because they are afraid to use their own. They're envious and, instead of finding constructive ways to feel engaged themselves, try to make you feel guilty or embarrassed for lacking their fear.

Believe in the power of the voice to change things! If you don't like the way a conversation is going, it is your responsibility as a listener-thinker-talker to try to turn it in another direction. This may sometimes take just a single sentence or a question—but if you remain a passive listener, waiting for some-one else to speak up, nothing may improve.

Develop the natural habit of talking to everybody everywhere, find all the flexible, various ways a voice may go, and the world will open up for you like a beautiful room.

24

GET HANDY
around the house

by Beverly DeJulio

The first thing that every girl should know about maintaining, improving, and decorating a home is that a girl *can* maintain and improve a home, not just decorate it!

When I was a young and recently divorced mom of four, I'd go to the hardware store to buy supplies for a project, and the men working there would ask why my husband wasn't purchasing the supplies.

"I *am* my husband!" was my terse reply.

Fortunately for today's girls, attitudes are changing. Just make sure *you* have the right attitude as well!

PUT TOGETHER A BASIC TOOL KIT

One of the first things to remember is that your most important tool for any project is sitting there between your ears! Collecting the proper information and planning ahead will save you lots of time and trouble in the long run.

That said, there are some basic tools that every home should have. When each one of my children left for college, I gave them a toolbox containing these basics. Of course, their first reaction when I handed them the toolbox was, "Mom, you know I'll be so busy studying I won't have time to use these tools!" (Did they think I was born yesterday? I only hoped they would do *some* studying!)

Funny thing was, each of them had several stories to tell about how handy the tools turned out to be. What they didn't realize before they arrived in the dorm room was how much they'd want to make the room look and feel like home. From hanging pictures to wiring in extension phone lines, from hanging curtains to building bunk or loft beds, there always seemed to be another project to pull out the old toolbox for. Since they were just about the only students with such a kit, everyone came knocking at their doors to borrow the tools. One daughter even related that it was a great way to meet guys!

EVERY HOME SHOULD HAVE A BASIC TOOL KIT WITH THE FOLLOWING:

- Hammer
- Pliers
- Screwdrivers
- Level
- Two sizes of adjustable wrenches
- Saw
- Tape measure
- Awl
- Safety glasses
- Plunger
- Utility knife
- Assortment of adhesives, including super glue, all-purpose glue, and a glue stick
- Assortment of tapes, including masking tape, duct tape, and electrical tape
- Thumbtacks
- Picture hangers
- Wire

In addition, my favorite power tools include a cordless drill and a saber saw. (While power tools are optional for college, they would be very necessary if you were going to be ambitious and build bunk beds or a shelving unit!)

LEARN TO HANDLE EMERGENCIES

Many of you may never do major home improvement projects like knocking down a wall to make a bigger room, remodeling a kitchen, or installing a new floor. However, knowing *nothing* about your home is a little like riding a bike with no hands. Things may go smoothly for a while, but as soon as you hit a bump, you're in big trouble! There are many things you need to know about taking care of your home, especially when there's an emergency.

Many emergencies have to do with plumbing and electrical problems. You may never fix a leaky faucet (although I'm sure with a little research and the right tools you could!) or install a chandelier, but you do need to know where the main shut-off valve for the plumbing and the main power box for the electricity are and how to operate them.

PLUMBING EMERGENCIES

Besides the main shut-off valve for the plumbing, most homes have shut-off valves at each sink, toilet, and appliance (automatic dishwasher, washing machine, etc.). This allows you to turn off the water (hot and cold) for that particular area of the home without interrupting service to the rest of the home.

Here are a few tips to file in the back of your mind—just in case!

A toilet has very few working parts, but when it's about to overflow, that really doesn't matter. All we can think about is all that water (possibly nasty water!) flooding the bathroom floor. Most toilets have a ball or canister-type float, which obviously floats on top of the water in the tank. The quickest way to keep the toilet from overflowing is to remove the tank lid and lift up on the float. That will temporarily stop the water from coming into the tank. Now prop something under the float to hold it up until you can turn the water off at the shut-off valve.

You may have heard that the plunger is a plumber's best friend. Well, it certainly is a necessary tool of the trade. In most cases, that's all you'll need to unclog a drain.

To prevent drains from clogging in the first place, use this simple recipe: About once a month, place a funnel in the sink drain and pour about a cup of baking soda and about a cup of hot white vinegar down the drain. Let it work overnight. The combination of baking soda and vinegar will loosen particles that are trying to make the trap (the U-shaped pipe under the sink) their home. (Warning: Do not use this mixture if your home has a septic tank—it could throw off the chemical balance.)

Now, a bathroom drain also presents another problem: hair.

If a bathroom drain is slow-flowing, the culprit is most likely a big, ugly, slimy hair blob. Many times, the plunger will not do the job since the hair may be tangled in the stopper mechanism. The best way to remove the hair blob is to get a brush with a long, flexible handle (available at pet, restaurant supply, and musical instrument stores). Slide the brush down the drain along the stopper until it won't go any farther and then twist the handle round and round. The hair will get tangled on the bristles and will come out when you pull the brush out of the drain.

ELECTRICAL EMERGENCIES

You need to know where the main power box for the house is. If an electrical circuit is overloaded or an appliance malfunctions, it will trigger that outlet's circuit breaker to turn off. Unplug the appliance that caused the problem and don't put it back into service until it has been repaired or replaced. For an overloaded circuit, either unplug some items or turn off some of the appliances or lights on the circuit. Once that's done, you can reset the breaker and flip it back on.

PROTECT YOUR HOME—AND YOURSELF

All homes should have *at least* one smoke detector and one carbon monoxide detector. It is important that you know how to test and change the batteries in each of them. (You should test them monthly and follow the manufacturer's instructions about replacing the batteries. For smoke detectors, it's normally recommended that you replace the batteries annually. A perfect time is every fall, when you set the clocks back to standard time.)

Every home should have a fire extinguisher on each level, and it should be stored near an exit for that level. That way, if the fire you're trying to extinguish gets out of control, you'll still be able to escape. Of course, first quickly assess the situation. If the smoke and fire are already out of control, exit the home and call the fire department from a neighbor's home or your cell phone. For fires that are just getting started, first call the fire department, then use the fire extinguisher. An easy way to remember how to use the extinguisher is to remember the word *PASS*. That will remind you to:

P: Pull the pin
A: Aim the nozzle
S: Squeeze the trigger
S: Sweep the base of the fire from side to side

LEARN TO CARE FOR FILTERS

There are several filters in different appliances around a home that need to be cleaned or replaced on a regular basis. Some that come to mind are the filters in the clothes dryer, the fan vent over a stove, the furnace, and the refrigerator.

One that many people either don't know about or ignore is the filter screen of a hair dryer. This filter can become so clogged that it can cause the dryer to overheat and, in some cases, burn out the motor. First, unplug the hair dryer! Then use a pair of tweezers to help pull the lint from the screen.

An overfilled bag or dirt cup can damage a vacuum cleaner's motor. Change the bag or empty the cup as needed.

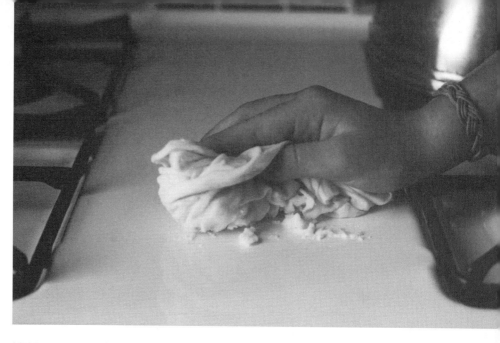

LEARN TO GET RID OF STAINS

See spot . . . see spot on the countertop . . . see spot on the furniture . . . see spot on the carpet . . . make spot go away! Here are a few of my favorite tips for getting rid of stains.

Most stains on countertops can be removed by sprinkling baking soda on a soft, damp cloth and rubbing the affected area. Rinse thoroughly and buff dry.

White rings on wooden furniture are caused when moisture gets trapped in the finish. There are many home remedies that will help. One that I've used for years is toothpaste (not the gel type) on a soft, damp cloth. Rub the area, going back and forth with the grain of the wood. This is enough of an abrasive to open the pores of the finish and allow the moisture to escape. Wipe the area with a damp cloth to remove the toothpaste residue, then apply furniture cream or polish. (I use a lemon oil furniture treatment available at hardware stores.)

TAKE CARE OF YOUR WALLS

If you never do any other project around your home, learning how to take care of the walls (and ceilings) not only will save you money, but also will help you add personality to your home. Painting is one of the least expensive ways to do this. You can totally change the look and feel of a room by changing the color of the walls and ceiling. This is also one of the easiest projects for a do-it-yourselfer. Hanging wallpaper borders, stenciling, rag rolling, sponging, or any other painting technique will really let you add your own personal touch.

But first, let me give you this warning: Don't just get out the paint can and start painting! There's lots of prep work that needs to be done first. You have to fill cracks, fix holes and popped nails, wash the walls, and prime newly patched or stained areas as well as newly installed drywall. Bottom line: Walls and ceilings need to be clean, smooth, and oil-free before you begin painting or hanging wall covering.

ADD PERSONALITY TO YOUR HOME

Learning to use tools can do more than help you handle emergencies. You can also have fun adding personality to your home by hanging photos, artwork, shelves, and window treatments. Just remember to attach any and all of these items to a wall stud when possible. When that's not possible, make sure you use the appropriate wall anchors for the weight of what is being hung.

Once you've learned to repair, maintain, and decorate your home, you'll save money and have lots of fun, too!

remember WHO YOU WANT TO BE

by Sara Shandler

I turned away from Geoff's Sandwich Shop, a staple eatery of my summer stay at a prestigious university, and bounced down a single step toward Emma. I clutched the bag containing the untouched half of my hummus sandwich—identical to Emma's—pleased I would have the leftovers of our delectable dinner to eat later.

"Shall we?" I asked, tilting my head in the general direction of the campus, a summer program folder tucked under my arm.

"No, wait!" Emma replied, her enthusiasm truly worthy of the exclamation point. "You'll never guess what I have."

I couldn't have guessed. Her unusually long fingers scurried through her wallet. Her curls hid the wallet as she leaned over it, then bounced up when she found what she was looking for, mirroring her excitement.

"Here. I found it."

She handed over a coupon for a free Milky Way Lite bar, redeemable for no more than sixty cents. A free candy bar: a small treat. But that is why I like Emma—we share genuine excitement over the smallest things. There is something so boring about people without passion, about people who don't get excited when they find a toy in their cereal box. Or who don't think really good chocolate is enough to make an evening. Or, for that matter, who don't get excited when they find couches in a movie theater, or overgrown gardens, or an orange-and-purple sunset that borders on amazing.

I like my life. I like people who like theirs, too.

I am oversimplifying, I suppose. Finding wonder in the trivial is not all I like in people. I admire another quality—a restless, penetrating mind. Those in my inner circle come with two qualifications: They appreciate the little things, and they question everything else. Emma qualified.

So I like Emma, and I didn't mind walking down to the CVS store so she could get her free candy bar. We crossed the street just left of the faded crosswalk. The evening air was cooler than usual. I gathered the material of my right sleeve into my left hand and slid my bare right arm inside my shirt. I did the same with my left sleeve, and buttoned the shirt up to the third button.

We walked along, commenting on how the dusk air seemed to wrap around us. The hum of conversation, whistles from some guys, and boisterous laughter from an outside restaurant provided a sound track for our escapade. In front of us, a couple held on to one another, each with a hand in the other's back pocket. The man turned toward his admirer and licked her forehead.

"Whatever floats your boat," I mumbled, loud enough for only Emma to hear. We laughed. In a gesture of self-consciousness, I placed my hand over my mouth to hide my smile.

At that moment I saw the puppy. Her paws were too big and her ears hung too long for the tiny body. Her eyes quietly peeked up from her oversized skin. I was so enthralled by her resemblance to my dog, Buber, that I stopped without a thought, taking no notice of her masters at first.

Had I looked at them initially, this would be a different essay or, probably, not an essay at all. In all likelihood, I would not have stopped. The evening would have made no impression on me.

But I did stop.

> I like
> my life.
> I like
> people
> who like
> theirs,
> too.

I don't remember what I did next. I remember the feeling only because I can still feel it as I struggle to articulate it here.

The puppy wagged her tail beside a beige Pinto, with its trunk open and a random collection of merchandise displayed inside. A family—mother, father, and little girl—eager to sell a necklace or bracelet or anklet or sweater or mittens stood in front of the mobile shop. It's not that I had an aversion to this family in particular. I rarely stop to examine the wares of street sellers, since I always feel obligated to buy something. Perhaps it's equally rude to keep walking, but leaving empty-handed after browsing seems even more like a personal affront to the hawker.

"They're selling all over the country, you know," said the father, pointing to a necklace rack. His braided gray hair rested neatly on his shoulder.

His wife reasserted his statement: "All over the country." They smiled, all three of them, saying how beautiful we'd look in one of the necklaces.

My limited summer budget didn't allow for many luxuries. Plus, I'd indulged in a new necklace just that morning. I told them so apologetically.

"You'd better buy an anklet, then," the wife said, leaning toward my leg to fasten one on.

Slightly resentful of the hard sell, I made another excuse, then commented on their puppy's good nature. (A safe bet. Surely she wasn't for sale.) Then I smiled and said thank you, preparing to walk away on a pleasant note.

The little girl, six or seven, and I made eye contact. She leaned on the dog and smiled, sticking her tongue through the gap in her teeth. I remembered receiving reimbursement from the tooth fairy for my own lost baby teeth. I waved good-bye, my cupped hand opening and closing.

She laughed and almost sang, "We have no money."

I don't remember what I did next. I remember the feeling only because I can still feel it as I struggle to articulate it here, some two and a half years later. My chest tightened. My breath was forced from the bottom of my stomach. My shoulders hunched around my emptied lungs.

The mother scolded the child, "That's not true, Regina."

Emma and I kept walking. I felt ashamed.

Up until now, writing this story has simply been a matter of trying to describe my evening. But here, here is where it gets difficult. You see, the evening was not as simple as a light dinner out and evening air. Our dinner conversation had been too fitting: Over our sandwiches, Emma and I had been discussing the air of entitlement that seems to accompany wealth. It was a very removed conversation, an intellectual discourse—certainly we were not like the people we discussed.

Emma had described a documentary she had watched in her sociology class. A group of European travelers went to an African village that had become a tourist attraction. The families in the village had lost their farmland and struggled to survive because of nearby industrialization. All hope of regaining their land was gone because of the escalating cost of real estate. In the face of hunger, the Europeans smiled and took pictures. "Look at the amusing people!" was their attitude. "How lucky they are that we are bringing our civilized ways to them."

As I pushed my falling sprouts back into my sandwich, I told her about my previous day. I walked back from class and saw a couple of acquaintances sauntering toward Paragon Grill, a relatively expensive off-campus restaurant. They invited me out to dinner. I told them that I was headed toward the Ratty, the dining hall, and asked them if they would like to join me. Monique, the young woman, flung her hair behind her shoulder and replied, "I don't do the Ratty."

"Eeew." Emma's comment expressed our mutual disgust. We self-righteously complained about other people's insensitivity and snobbery.

I found a twisted pride in telling Emma about the scene my rusted 1986 Honda Civic station wagon made upon my arrival at the program that June. My little blue bomb had overheated, steamed, and boiled over while parallel-parked between a convertible BMW and a deep green Jaguar.

We basked in our difference from the other summer program participants— unlike them, we did "do the Ratty."

At that self-congratulatory moment, the facts of my own privilege had escaped me. I was spending my summer eating in an Ivy League university's cafeteria; I had to do little more than ask my parents nicely for the thousands of dollars my time there would cost. My little overheating disaster was my car, which I owned. This little girl, with her gapped teeth and unintentionally powerful words, provided an intense check for my self-congratulation that night; now, more than two years later, she still does.

I've been especially privileged, but economic prosperity is not the only type of advantage. All of us are privileged in at least three very important ways: We are young, we have a future, and we can still choose to make a difference.

To this day, I hold the details of that evening—the smell of the summer air, the contents of my sandwich, the type of candy bar, the loose-skinned puppy, and gap-toothed Regina—as reminders of what I take for granted, of who I am and who I want to be in this world. No little girl with overgrown bangs and a gap in her teeth should go to bed hungry.

Remember who you are and who you want to be. Just as important, remember who you *don't* want to be. Most important, remember that you can make a difference. Do better than I did that summer night.

Emma and I walked silently away from the man, woman, gap-toothed cherub, and frisky puppy. We arrived at our destination—CVS. Inside, pop music resonated all around us. Emma found the Milky Way Lite bar and handed it to the cashier with her coupon.

"That'll be four cents, miss. You have to pay for the tax."

"Oh." Emma handed over a nickel. "Here you go. Thanks."

"Have a nice day, ladies."

26

WRITE AN ETHICAL WILL:
A LETTER TO MY TO MY DAUGHTER

by Laura Scher

Dear Alison,

Our Jewish heritage has a wonderful tradition called writing an "ethical will." But it's not like a will in the movies where someone dies and children get money, jewelry, or a big ranch. This will is about passing on things that last a whole lot longer. It's about passing on values that you hold dear and that you want your children to have, too.

As I grew up, I learned that believing in your dreams and having a generous spirit are much more important than anything money can buy. These are the things I want you to inherit. These are the things I want you to treasure as you grow up.

Your grandparents raised me to believe I could do whatever I wanted to do, be whoever I wanted to be. And you can, too.

Remember when the genie tells Aladdin that he can do anything except make people fall in love with him? It's true. You can never make people do what you want. And you can never tell them what to think of you. But when

you respect people and remain true to yourself, you will be surprised at all the great things that will happen.

I was never popular in high school. I wore braces from the tenth grade through my freshman year in college. In those days, we didn't have fun-colored braces and rubber bands. Our teeth really did look like big railroad tracks. But as shy as I was, I learned to stop being embarrassed and just laugh out loud when I heard something that was really funny.

I never let my disappointments hold me back. In school plays, I wasn't chosen for the big parts, so I volunteered to make costumes instead. I wasn't elected editor in chief of the newspaper, so I worked as a reporter. I was a terrible athlete armed with a permanent excuse from gym class, but I joined the swim team and swam third string. At the end of the year, I was shocked to be elected president of the extracurricular honor society. Even though I was never the star, people noticed I was willing to be involved—and they respected me for it. I also learned that if I stuck with something, I could push myself to the next level. You can make your dreams happen when you break them down into small pieces.

I also learned to love math, and I hope you will, too. In the beginning, it's all about memorizing facts. But after that, it's all about solving problems. You might not think of math as fun now, but coming up with solutions to hard problems is so fun and creative that you learn to love solving all the problems that come up in your life.

Striving to do whatever you want to do doesn't end after school. When I graduated from Harvard's business school, I didn't want to work for a company devoted to inventing a new cereal. I wanted to help build a company that could change the lives of millions of people. I wanted to be part of a business that supported peace, freedom, and a clean environment around the world. That's why I founded Working Assets, a long-distance, credit-card, and online services company that donates part of the money it makes to nonprofit groups working for peace, human rights, equality, education, and the environment.

We faced a lot of hurdles in creating our business. The critics told us that a company had to be dedicated to making money above everything else. Otherwise, it wouldn't last. We proved them wrong. I founded the company in 1985, and not only is it still here, but it's donated more than $20 million to nonprofit groups since then.

We learn so much about ourselves and the world by being generous. Already you're giving part of your allowance to walkathons for cancer or AIDS, and I hope that when you are older, you will give a part of your salary to charities, family members, or a particular homeless person who touches you.

Sharing our good fortune rewards us in ways we can't measure. Remember your ninth birthday party, when we all cooked something that everyone loved? Later, I think we all agreed that the most fun was donating the food to a family shelter.

But having a generous spirit goes beyond giving. It means thinking about others as much as ourselves. It means giving up a Saturday to help clean up a park, spending time with an elderly relative, comforting a friend who has just lost a job, or visiting a friend who has just had a baby. I was especially proud of you when you had a sleepover and invited a girl who didn't have a lot of friends at school. She wasn't a good friend, but she needed to be asked. That's generosity.

And finally, I want you to know that *values* is not just a fancy word. Values form the deepest part of our lives and guide us through our everyday activities. As you grow older they will become more defined, but even as a fourth-grader you already have a strong sense of right and wrong. You have a strong sense of fairness. You are aware of your impact on others and the world around you. Having good values means having respect for the environment, for recycling, planting trees, or working in a garden.

So you see, Alison, this is my ethical will to you. By being true to yourself, following your dreams, and keeping a generous spirit, you can do whatever you set your heart on doing. And be whoever you want to be.

Love,
Mom

SIMPLIFY YOUR LIFE

by Cecile Andrews

When I was in the eighth grade, I had an experience that changed my life. We had just finished an exciting game of volleyball, and my team had won—thanks to me. So I was feeling pretty good as I walked out of the gym. But as I was heading for the showers, my PE teacher called me over. "Cecile," she said, "you've got to quit being so loud and noisy or the boys won't like you. You must learn to be more ladylike and poised."

I was shocked and stunned. I could feel my face get red as I stood there trying not to cry.

What did she mean, the boys wouldn't like me? The boys liked me fine! I always had a boyfriend, and I always got asked to dance at school dances.

But she was my teacher. Perhaps she knew something. So I decided to try. For the next several years, I tried to be more ladylike, but somehow things kept . . . happening. When I was playing my flute in band, I fell off the risers. When I walked to the front of the class, I tripped or knocked something off the teacher's desk. When my friends told funny jokes, I couldn't help laughing—loudly.

Finally, I gave up. I could see that it was useless for me to try to be more ladylike. Besides, I could also see that it didn't work; the boys liked me better when I was myself.

That was a long time ago, but what I discovered is still true. Everyone likes you better when you're being yourself!

You may find, however, that you're being told that you have to be different by a voice that's even louder and more powerful than my teacher's voice. Today, we're constantly bombarded by ads that tell us that what's important in life is being popular, wearing nice clothes, and driving a fancy car. And to have those things, you have to be the kind of person you see in commercials. You have to pretend to be someone you're not.

We're told that we must be thin, be pretty, and smile all the time. We're told to change our looks and our personalities. We're constantly told, just as that teacher told me, that what and who we are is not acceptable.

Those commercials are really just another version of my PE teacher telling me to be a phony instead of someone real. They tell you to conform. They try to manipulate you into being true to their brand instead of true to yourself. They tell you that there's something wrong with you and that you need to "fix" yourself—not through personal growth or by looking within, but by buying something. They tell girls that they are too fat, that their hair is wrong, that they don't have the right body. They never suggest that the secret to life is being true to yourself.

Unfortunately, we're so surrounded by these messages that sometimes we don't even realize what's going on. Teenage girls have told me about having been teased by other kids if they were not wearing expensive brand-name clothing. Some were told that their clothes were cheap and stupid! One girl said she felt like an outcast because she couldn't afford the clothes others were wearing.

The constant message to buy, buy, buy does more than hurt your self-esteem. It can also keep you from living the life you'd like.

For example, I was talking to a group of kids one day about what kind of life they wanted when they grew up. They all said that they didn't want to work all the time. They didn't like the fact that their parents were never around, so they wanted more time to spend with their kids. But they were worried about how they could make enough money to support a family if they only worked part time. They also worried about what the planet would be like in their future. Would they be able to breathe fresh air and drink clean water?

Ironically, both worries are rooted in the same problem: extreme consumerism. The more we buy, the more we have to work and the less free time we have. The more we buy, the more we destroy the planet by creating trash and wasting natural resources.

But some people are rebelling. I work with something called the Voluntary Simplicity movement, a movement that has been called one of the top ten trends of the nineties. It's a movement that questions the idea that more is better—in fact, it argues that less is more. The people involved in the Voluntary Simplicity movement have found that having lots of money doesn't necessarily make them happy. They would rather have more time than more money. They would rather forge a closer connection to nature than own lots of stuff. It's not self-deprivation. It's figuring out what is really important.

So, what can you do? Here's a seven-point plan for creating a simpler life that lets you follow your dreams and be true to yourself.

1 REDUCE YOUR CONSUMERISM.

Every time you want to buy something, write it down in a little notebook. Wait a week and take another look at what you wrote. Then ask yourself if you still want it. A lot of times you don't care anymore!

If you do still want it, ask yourself these questions:

• Can you use something else? First, try to find a way to get the thing you want without buying it. Is there something lying around the house you can use instead?

- Can you borrow it? Does your sister or mother have something you can use?
- Can you trade something for it?
- Can you rent it? People going to a fancy dance can often rent an expensive dress instead of buying a dress they may only wear one time.
- Can you buy it used at a thrift store, a consignment shop, or a garage sale?
- If you need to buy it new, can you buy it at a little local store? If everyone shops at big discount chains, interesting small stores will go out of business.
- What effect will your purchase have on the environment? Look at the amount of packaging used for the product. Ask yourself if it is biodegradable. Does it contain toxins? How far was it shipped? Transportation means burning oil and polluting the environment. Why should we buy something that was made in China when someone in our state might make it just as well?
- Finally, ask yourself who made it. Is it a big corporation that pays sweatshop wages to children in other countries? (You can find out by doing research at the library or on the Internet.) Vote for justice with your dollars!

After asking all these questions, you may not even be interested in buying whatever it was. If you don't buy it, congratulate yourself. You have saved some money and helped save the planet.

2 PUT YOUR TV IN THE CLOSET.

By the time teenagers graduate from high school, many will have watched more than 350,000 commercials. (In fact, the average American spends an entire year of his or her life watching TV commercials.)

But sometimes it's just so easy to sit in front of the TV and escape from the day. Help yourself resist by putting your TV somewhere that makes watching it difficult—like a closet. When there's something good to watch, you can get it out. When you don't have a TV staring you in the face, you're more likely to do something that boosts your self-esteem, like playing your guitar or drawing cartoons. And you won't become a commercial model wanna-be.

3 RESIST COMMERCIALISM IN SCHOOLS.

Even if you never watch TV, you'll still probably see a lot of ads and commercials in a place you might not expect—your school! For example, you may see:

- Ads posted in school halls, school buses, or classrooms
- A company giving out feminine hygiene samples to junior-high girls
- *Channel One,* the free TV news program for schools that includes two minutes of ad time
- Soft drink companies giving schools money in return for exclusive rights to sell and promote their products
- A free curriculum kit featuring brand-name candy bars
- Free book covers plastered with ads
- Corporate names on sports equipment, scoreboards, and uniforms

However, many individuals and organizations want to make schools commercial-free zones. For instance, people recently protested a proposal that would have let Pepsi place its logo in a Berkeley school's sports facilities. The school board then voted to ban all advertising and logos—no ads in instructional materials and no logos on sports uniforms or equipment.

(Don't wait for adults to fix things. The Berkeley protest campaign was started by a fifteen-year-old girl who organized a student-led forum.)

4 DON'T BLINDLY CONFORM TO FASHION.

Fashion is a way that society can control you. Why should the "fashion experts" tell you how to dress? Kids everywhere are buying used clothes or trading stuff they already have. At Evergreen State College in Olympia, Washington, students get their clothes free, out of a box. When they're tired of wearing something, they throw it in the box and rummage through to find something new to them. (It's a great way to meet people. You never know when someone will come up to you and say, "Hey! You look great in that shirt! It used to be mine!")

5 REFUSE TO BE A BILLBOARD.
If companies want you to advertise their products, they should be paying you! Why should you walk around with corporate logos plastered all over your body? Look for clothes without logos or find old clothes that don't have a brand name. (They used to put the brand names in places you couldn't see them!) Some kids wear their clothes inside out so they don't have to be a walking commercial.

6 SAVE YOUR MONEY.
Everything in our society is telling you to buy, buy, buy. But if you start saving now, you could have a lot of money by the time you reach thirty.

Now, I'm not suggesting that you save your money just so you can buy more things. What you will be able to buy, someday, is more freedom. A lot of people are saving their money so that they can afford to work part time, start their own business, or do work they love that doesn't pay very much.

For instance, if you spend one dollar a day on candy or soda, that adds up to $365 a year. If you saved that $365 in a savings account that earned 5 percent a year, it would grow to $465.84 by the end of five years. By the end of thirty years, you would have $1,577.50.

Of course, as you get older, you'll save much more than a dollar a day, and by that time you'll be in the habit of saving money. And as you get older, you can learn more about investing your money, and you might get an even higher rate of interest!

7 FIND YOUR PASSION.

Instead of preparing for a high-paying, high-status job, focus on finding a career that you love. (If following your passion leads to a high-paying, high-status job, great! But don't sell out your dreams for a job that you think you *should* take just because you'll make lots of money.) People who are involved with their passion almost never want to spend time at the mall or in front of their television.

Just a few final words. What is it we really want out of life? To have a good time and make a difference. That's the promise of the Voluntary Simplicity movement.

write your name ON A WALL

By Lois Lowry

Most of the time, the two-hundred-year-old farmhouse that we own in the country sits there empty, as if it were asleep. But some weekends, and many vacations, we fill it with friends and family and it seems to wake, to breathe again with life.

Old as it is, the house has needed attention. This fall, we hired a contractor to do a lot of work: new roof, new wiring, new plaster on the walls, new paint.

Last week, he called me.

"Found a message inside a wall," he said. "Left there by a little boy a long time ago."

I was astonished. But my contractor wasn't. "Happens a lot," he told me. "I find 'em all the time."

My little long-ago boy was eleven, and his name was Norman. He wrote his message on a wooden beam (I had hoped for a folded paper that we could frame and hang on a wall), so now it is sealed back up, hidden there behind the plaster once again. But Norman inhabits my house now, and I like having him there.

I lived in many houses when I was young. Honolulu, New York, Pennsylvania, Tokyo. Some of them I have never seen again. One of them— the Tokyo house—has been torn down. When I went back two years ago, I saw only a grassy park where my house had been.

The Pennsylvania house still stands, but it is owned by a college now. I returned once, peered through a window, and saw that the room where the piano had been, the room where the Christmas tree had stood, now contained desks and computers. It made me sad. I wondered if the people who sat working at those computers knew that the house had once been home to a little girl. Upstairs, in a back bedroom—now an office—I had looked down into a bassinet to meet my newborn brother for the first time, in 1943.

There was a closet in that back bedroom that had shelves so deep, so enormous, that my sister and I used them as a human dollhouse. We each claimed a shelf as our living space and furnished it with treasures. We could actually climb up, sit on our respective shelf-floors, and hold tea parties and conversations. I thought we should try sleeping in the closet, on our shelves, but my sister said no. She thought it would be scary.

I suppose those shelves are now cluttered with files and office supplies. Secretaries probably step in to find some document or a stack of fresh paper for the copying machine. They have no idea that they are trespassing, stepping briefly into the world of imagination where a child once lived.

How I wish I had written my name somewhere in that closet. How I wish someone would see it there and become aware of a long-ago me.

In my book *A Summer to Die,* a young girl named Meg meets an elderly man who grew up in the house where she now lives.

"The little room was mine," he says, "when I was a small boy. Sometime when your father isn't working there, go in and look in the closet. On the closet floor you'll find my name carved."

In *Anastasia Again!* the Krupnik family prepares to move away from the apartment where Anastasia, now twelve, has lived her entire life. Anastasia finds a pencil stub in the trash can. She kneels on the bare floor in a corner of the room and writes on the wallpaper, in her best printing: "This is my room forever. Anastasia Krupnik."

There is a house in Falmouth, Maine, with pale yellow wallpaper in the living room. Someday, when someone scrapes off that wallpaper, an elaborate cartoon drawing will be exposed. It is signed by my son, Ben, who was about thirteen at the time he drew it there on the bare plaster, with my permission.

Ben is a grown man now, married, with a child of his own. But his childhood self lives forever in that house. Tomorrow, or five years from tomorrow, or ten years after that, a stranger will look at his drawing and his name, smile, and say, "Hi, Ben." And for a moment that young boy will live again, smiling back, making the connection between generations.

Write your name on a wall in the house where you live today, when you are young. Find a place in the attic, in the basement, in a closet. Use an indelible pen. Use your best handwriting.

Then go on with your life. Grow up and go away. Get a job, marry, and have children. Grow old. Forget about your childhood self and who you were, a long time ago.

But someday in the future, some stranger, a person not yet born, will find your name there, smile, and whisper hi, and a long-ago you will be alive forever.

29

FOLLOW LIFE'S SIGNPOSTS

N

W

S

by Chely Wright

Let me first say that I truly do not have life figured out. I'm twenty-nine years old and single, with no children. So, as you can imagine, my experiences are a bit limited.

However, I have lived quite an exciting life so far. And the one constant has been hard work and staying focused on the goals I've set for myself. I was seventeen when I left my small Kansas hometown to pursue my dream of a recording career. (The dream that I announced to the world when I was three!) And my overnight success took twelve years, since I just received my first gold record this year.

To some, the entertainment industry may seem like quite a glamorous life. I've found that the reality is that glamour is the smallest piece of the pie— that hard work, long hours, and work schedules that go way beyond the nine-to-five standard are the norm. After all, it is called show *business*.

As I've traveled the road of life, I've watched for signposts to help me stay on track. If someday I do have a daughter, I'll share with her the following list that I compiled with the help of my sister, Jennifer Archer.

1. **D**on't do anything to or with your body that you wouldn't want your grandma to know about.

2. **W**rite more thank-you notes than you receive.

3. **G**et up to see the sunrise every chance you get!

4. **J**ust because you were once something doesn't necessarily mean that you will remain that. For example: nail biter, geek, overeater, the most popular, a slob, a clean freak, the prettiest, the most unattractive.

5. **S**omeone in this great big world will love you exactly the way you are—and you should, too.

6. **A**lways keep a stamp and a ten-dollar bill hidden somewhere in your checkbook.

7. **D**on't smoke cigarettes—if not to protect your health, then so my loved ones and I won't have to smell the smoke in a restaurant.

8. **B**e able to cook at least one meal really well.

9. **I**f you're on a self-destructive path, you'll probably be one of the last to find out about it. Listen to your mother!

10. **I**f you notice that someone has made an effort to look nice, compliment them.

11. **C**onsider this: The person that you intentionally cut off in traffic might turn out to be your emergency-room doctor later in the day.

12. **A**lways buy Girl Scout cookies and lemonade from anyone under the age of twelve. (I strongly recommend Thin Mints. They are Band-Aids for your heart.)

13. **I**f someone wants to talk to you about their religious beliefs, let them. You might learn something, and they might, too.

14. **R**espect the elderly. You may be roommates sooner than you expect.

15. Even Tyra Banks looks in the mirror and sees things she would change. Give yourself a break!

16. If you don't want people to call you a liar, don't tell lies.

17. Put lotion on your feet before you go to bed.

18. Remember, nothing lasts forever, including (1) beauty, (2) employment, (3) pleasure, (4) pain, (5) youth, and (6) the flu.

19. Appreciate your brothers and sisters. Your relationships with them will be the closest, truest, and longest ones in your life.

20. Any price is negotiable. (Remember that nine-year-old at the lemonade stand? Chances are she'll come down a nickel!)

21. Regarding business and dreams: Every "no" means you are that much closer to a "yes."

22. Approach constructive criticism as another tool in your tool belt. This doesn't mean that you always have to use it.

23. Go all out to celebrate the holidays: decorate, sing, wear silly sweatshirts, and spend time with people you care about.

24. Always let someone take your picture. The older you get, the more you'll appreciate the sentimental value of those photos. Not to mention that your family will always cherish them.

25. No matter how much money you have, you never have so much that you don't need to use coupons.

30

TAKE CONTROL OF YOUR HEALTH

By Barbara Seaman

If you haven't yet, soon you may be visiting doctors and other health care providers on your own. Women's attitudes toward doctors have changed quite drastically since I was a girl. We used to be urged to blindly follow their advice. ("Doctor's orders! Don't worry your pretty little head about it. Let the doctor do the worrying for you. Would he give you anything that would hurt you?") Now we know there are many times when we must question doctors, because with all their good intentions they often do just what kids do—namely, they follow fads. We shouldn't accept their prescriptions or advice until we're convinced they make sense. We should tell them, "Show me."

Here's an example: When I was 16, my doctor suggested I could easily lose weight if I would "reach for a cigarette following each meal, instead of dessert. Three cigarettes could never harm you."

Once hooked, how many people could limit themselves to three cigarettes daily? Not me. Later, another doctor swore to me that infant formula was "nutritionally superior" to breast milk. He did all he could to talk me out of breast-feeding, because he fully—but also naively—believed the sales pitch of the formula company representatives. I would caution you to be a little bit suspicious of any doctor who wants you to follow what sounds like an unnatural course for a normal, healthy condition, i.e. when you are not ill.

One thing I mercifully did refuse was X-ray treatments a skin doctor ordered for my acne when I was in high school. The treatment didn't even work that well, from what I could see—and years later two of the kids I knew who were treated by him died from cancers that were said to result from this misguided acne Rx.

Therefore I tell my granddaughters Sophia, nine, and Idalia, six, "When it comes to health, don't just drift along in life. Pick up the paddle! Say, 'Show me . . . explain this . . . justify that.' You have every right to understand what people (including doctors) are telling you to do to *your* body."

Never let doctors patronize you or make you feel stupid or small. Demand respect. Promise to never tolerate high-handed, inconsiderate behavior, brusque or evasive answers to questions, exams where you feel ignored, overly intimate or embarrassing talk or touching. If an authority treats you badly and you reveal it to your friends, you'll often find that some of them have had similar experiences. Don't blame yourself. Some professionals simply aren't fit for their jobs. When you encounter those who are good at what they do, try to keep them.

There will be many times in your life when you'll need to question doctors and take charge of your health. But you need to take your first big step in that area right now, and the health issue that should concern you is . . . calcium.

Sound boring? It's not! In fact, if you plan to be a healthy adult, you must take steps in that direction now. I mean *right now,* because scientists have

"When I was 16 my doctor suggested I could easily lose weight if I would 'reach for a cigarette following each meal.'"

learned that the four years surrounding puberty (generally ten to fourteen in girls and twelve to sixteen in boys) are *the most crucial* for developing lifelong healthy bones. A whopping 35 to 40 percent *of all the bone mass you will ever have* is laid down during this four-year interval.

When you hit your forties, you'll start to lose bone mineral. But if you make ample "deposits" into your "personal bone account" now, you'll probably have the needed reserves to draw upon later in life. It's like saving money for a rainy day—or, as Sophia said, "We should think like a squirrel hoarding nuts for the winter, but in our case it's not nuts—it's calcium."

Some things—and I maintain that healthy eating is among them—are best discussed grandparent to kid. When parents talk to kids, food conversations are apt to explode into an unproductive power struggle. My grandkids know that at my house they're allowed to have more . . . um . . . delicacies . . . than in their own kitchens. So when I pitched calcium to Sophia, she was surprised but receptive.

Sophia likes to do her own research, and I hope you feel the same. There are so many conflicting health claims and products out there that every girl should take the time to be choosy and informed. As a science reporter, I had plenty of newsletters, charts, and government advisories on hand to help Sophia learn more about calcium. She learned that a most trustworthy source, the Institute of Medicine of the National Academy of Sciences, now recommends the following calcium intake:

➤ Ages four to eight years old: 800mg/day
➤ Ages nine to eighteen years old: 1,300mg/day
➤ Ages nineteen to fifty years old: 1,000mg/day
➤ Ages over fifty years old: 1,200mg/day

Imagine—Sophia is only four feet two inches tall and weighs only fifty-six pounds. However, she just turned nine as I write this, so from now until her high school graduation she will need more calcium than at any other stage in her life.

But only one in four boys and one in ten girls between the ages of nine and eighteen actually maintain their recommended daily intake of 1,300 mg, according to the National Institutes of Health. (The average American consumes less than 800 mg of calcium a day.)

Even worse, many girls not only neglect high-calcium foods and beverages, such as milk, but select substitutes, such as diet cola.

So how does a girl get her intake up to 1,300 mg a day?

At first, Sophia was discouraged when she studied my tables on the calcium content of different foods. Reluctantly she said she'd try to drink two cups of milk each day, instead of one, which would bring her to 600 mg, or almost halfway. She brightened when she realized that instead of the second glass of milk she could have a yogurt, and all but glowed to discover that two glasses of fortified juice would take her to 1,000 mg.

She also enjoys tofu, mozzarella, and some of the calcium-rich vegetables, such as broccoli. She chokes on pills, but she's tried some of the chewable supplements, and she likes them okay. She'll aim for getting 1,000 mg daily from food and making up the rest in supplements. (Supplements are good, but real food is better.)

In the course of our research, Sophia and I found the following tips on selecting and taking supplements:

• The sellers of many competing products, with mysterious chemical names such as calcium carbonate, calcium citrate, calcium gluconate, calcium lactate, or calcium phosphate, claim that they are best for you or give you the most for your money. To figure out which product is actually best, Sophia and I turned to the trusted, nonprofit (it doesn't receive money from drug companies) *Medical Letter on Drugs and Therapeutics.*

Although calcium carbonate contains the most elemental calcium, it also causes the most discomfort and is the most indigestible. Thus, current evaluators say, a dosage of calcium carbonate actually delivers *less* of the daily requirement than the same dosage of calcium citrate, which is deemed most digestible, lowest in side effects, and therefore the best bet. Everyone's body has its own peculiarity, however (or hadn't you noticed?), so if you find a product other than citrate that suits you, there is probably no need to switch. However, another drawback to carbonate is that some brands may contain traces of lead.

Thousands of Web sites offer health information. We have selected four that girls have said they liked:

1. ASK AMY
www.feminist.com
Amy Richards is co-author of *Manifesta: Young Women, Feminism and the Future.* (F,S,&G .2000). She is also affiliated with *MS. Magazine* in New York City and The Third Wave organization. At this Web site, she answers questions on subjects such as body image, health, and relationships.

1. NATIONAL WOMEN'S HEALTH NETWORK
www.womenshealthnetwork.org
Founded in 1975 in Washington, D.C., "NWHN" is the only national public interest membership organization dedicated exclusively to women's health. It does not accept financial support from pharmaceutical companies, tobacco companies, or medical device manufacturers. It offers internships—where students can learn about activism and advocacy—and aims to provide unbiased information on hundreds of (often-controversial) health topics.

CALCIUM CONTENT OF SOME FOODS*

Food Serving Size Calcium Content (mg)

Milk, skim [1 cup] 302

Yogurt (low-fat, fruit-flavored) [8 ounces] 300

Gruyère cheese [1 ounce] 287

Swiss cheese [1 ounce] 272

Figs, dried [10 figs] 269

Tofu, raw, firm [½ cup] 258

Calcium-fortified cereal [¾ cup] 250

Cheddar cheese [1 ounce] 204

Calcium-fortified orange juice [6 ounces] 200

Mozzarella, part skim [1 ounce] 183

Collard greens, cooked from frozen, chopped [½ cup] 179

American cheese, processed [1 ounce] 174

Blackstrap molasses [1 tablespoon] 172

Creamed cottage cheese [1 cup] 126

Sardines, canned in oil [2 sardines] 92

Parmesan cheese, grated [1 tablespoon] 69

Mustard greens [½ cup] 52

Kale, boiled [½ cup] 47

Broccoli, boiled [½ cup] 36

*From *J.A.T. Pennington, Bowes and Church's Food Values of Portions Commonly Used*, 17th ed. (Philadelphia : Lippincott, 1998.) Printed in *The Medical Letter on Drugs and Therapeutics*, Vol. 42 (issue 1075), April 3, 2000.

• Taking calcium with food and in doses of 500 mg or less increases absorption (the amount of calcium your body can actually take in at once).

• In nature, calcium usually pairs up with magnesium in a ratio of two to one. For that reason, some nutritionists prefer supplements that provide magnesium along with the calcium in the same two-to-one ratio.

• Calcium cannot be well utilized without vitamin D, so when sun is absent, be sure that your foods are enriched with vitamin D, or take a supplement.

• We also found some really good news. Some girls report an immediate bonus from calcium. Premenstrual syndrome (PMS) and cramps can be reduced if you take calcium supplements, along with taking B vitamins and vitamin C, cutting down on salty food, and consuming more food and drinks that are naturally "diuretic" (meaning they draw out water or make you want to pee). Some examples of diuretic foods are cranberry juice, rose hip tea and eggplant. Also, it may be hard to force yourself to exercise when you are crampy, but it can really help. And exercise also helps build bone mass. All in all, what's good for your bones may also relieve menstrual pain.

I hope that all granddaughters everywhere take their calcium, question authority when it doesn't make sense, locate doctors who earn and deserve their trust, and stay healthy long enough to love and enjoy their grandchildren to the fullest. Then they'll know that while there is no free lunch in life, there is free dessert.

And while we're on that delicious topic—dessert—here's some information that is oft omitted from the scientific tables on the calcium content of food. According to the *New York Times*, a cup of vanilla soft-serve ice cream contains (hooray!) 236 mg of calcium. . . . You can count that in.

3. OFFICE OF RESEARCH ON WOMEN'S HEALTH / OFFICE OF SCIENCE EDUCATION AT NATIONAL INSTITUTES OF HEALTH
science-education.nih. gov/col/
This site, based in Maryland, offers inspiration for girls who are thinking of careers in medicine and science. It includes information on minority health issues and inherited patterns of disease, plus an interactive curriculum in English and Spanish.

4. OUR BODIES, OURSELVES FOR THE NEW CENTURY
www.ourbodiesourselves.org
The Boston Women's Health Book Collective started publishing—and updating—the book *Our Bodies, Ourselves* in 1970, which provides information to help women and girls take more health matters into their own hands. OBOS—as it is nicknamed—is now an international switchboard for information and activism.

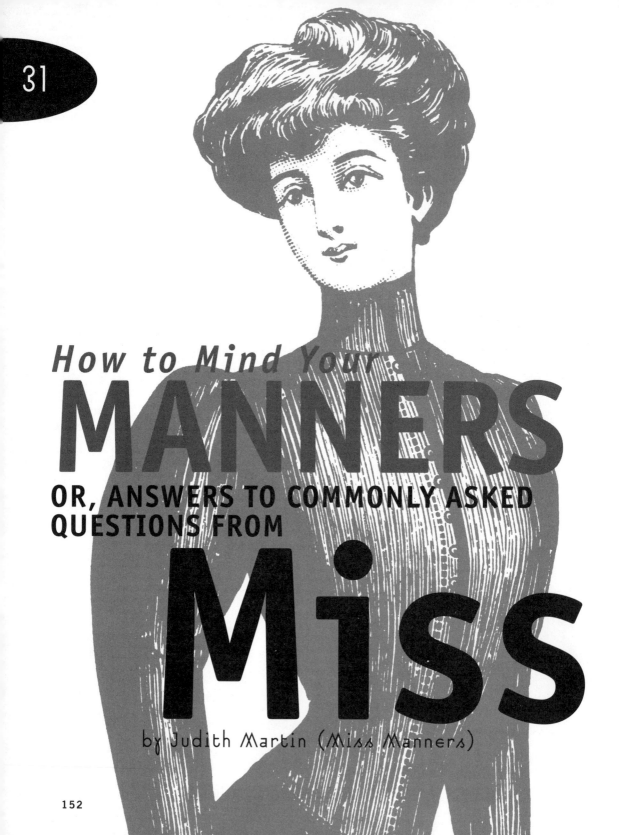

31

How to Mind Your
MANNERS
OR, ANSWERS TO COMMONLY ASKED QUESTIONS FROM
Miss

by Judith Martin (Miss Manners)

Dear Miss Manners—At my high school, there is a dance where the girls ask the guys, and about a month and a half ago, I asked a friend to go and he said yes. At the same time, a girl friend of mine asked a guy that both of us had a crush on (she first asked me if it was okay) and he said yes, as well.

My friend's date is now my boyfriend.

All my friends say that I should explain to my date, who is friends with my boyfriend, that I am now going to this dance with my boyfriend, and he will understand. My girl friend holds my date in passionate dislike, and refuses to swap dates, but she says she can easily get another date.

I contend that I should go with my original date and my boyfriend should go with my friend, for the sake of etiquette. Besides, I am looking forward to dancing with my friend, and I plan to dance mostly with him—but of course, I will dance one or two slow dances with my boyfriend.

Gentle Reader—Did you say "for the sake of etiquette"? Miss Manners has to still her fluttering heart.

It is not just that you recognize that etiquette—and not just your preferences—must be considered. What thrills her even more is that you understand not only the rule of etiquette, but the mannerly principle underlying it.

The rule is: Never cancel a social engagement because a better one comes along—even one so much better a one as romance.

Manners'
GENTLE YOUNG READERS

This rule exists not only because canceling disrupts the plans of others, but because it hurts their feelings. However much they may claim to "understand"—and what else can a rejected person say?—they do not.

Or rather, they understand only too well that you have deserted them for something better. (Being deserted for something worse—illness—is something they do understand.) This dampens a friendship, and you appear to have a very nice friendship with your date.

Miss Manners has only one thing to add to your masterful solution:

Would you consider going into the etiquette business after you finish your education?

Dear Miss Manners—I have noticed that when friends call me up for homework assignments or other things, they will ask for the information and, as I begin to give it, interrupt to say, "Hang on—I need a pencil and paper."

I admit I have been guilty of doing this, but am trying to have all my writing utensils ready, now that I realize what a pain it is to the person on the other end.

Am I just being picky? This has been bugging me for a while.

Gentle Reader—Miss Manners identifies with you (she always knows what the homework is, and she always has pencil and paper at every telephone, too), and this entitles you to refer to your feeling as proper, rather than picky.

Although she would prefer that you be generously tolerant, and use the time when your friends go for their supplies to reflect that life ultimately rewards those who know the homework, she wants to allow you some relief. If you promise to use a polite tone, you may respond, "That's okay, just call me back when you're ready."

Dear Miss Manners—My boyfriend and I got into a fight because he doesn't think it is right or polite, but thinks it is rude, to kiss me in the hallways at school.

Mostly everyone else does it too, but I also feel that it is wrong to show a lot of public affection around school. I want to know if you think it is polite to kiss and hug someone in public, especially at school.

Gentle Reader—First Miss Manners has a question: What are you fighting about?

Your boyfriend thinks it is rude to kiss in school hallways. You also think it is wrong to do so. What is the problem?

Miss Manners gathers it is that you think he ought to do it anyway for the purpose of impressing other people whose standard of behavior is lower than both of yours. This is not a good way to figure the right thing to do.

Kissing in front of other people is vulgar because it invites those people to become an audience to intimacy. Romancing couples like to do this because they assume that such an audience will be envious and admiring.

But their audiences are more critical than they imagine. Their actual entertainment consists of asking hilariously what the lovers can possibly see in each other and of noting gleefully any subsequent signs that the romance is faltering.

Dear Miss Manners—I am a 14-year-old who has had a lot of experience baby-sitting, and I hope you have suggestions that will be of help to me as well as others sharing my concerns.

One of my clients paid me for half of the hour and another family paid me for three hours instead of the four I worked! I would like to have a tactful way of letting them know I don't find this an acceptable way to pay for the quality care I give to their children.

What should (or can) I do when they are late, say an hour or so?

I have always smiled and overlooked it, but when they act as if their "reasons" excuse the inconvenience caused to me, it is disturbing.

When they are late, it forces me to lose out on valuable sleep, especially on school nights, and they don't pay "overtime."

Is it rude to tell my clients that I prefer to have the mother, not the father, drive me home?

Gentle Reader—Miss Manners sees that you need a lesson in business manners, starting with the fact that there is such a thing. While she appreciates the fact that you have preferred hurting your business to seeming rude, even though you resent that choice, she can assure you that this sacrifice is not necessary.

If you were doing a one-time favor for friends, social manners would require you to forgive their lapses while resolving not to be caught by them again. Business manners allow you to call attention to their failure to live up to the bargain and to indicate that you cannot work under such conditions.

Note that Miss Manners is not saying that doing business entitles you to be rude. An unfortunate number of business people, and the clients and customers with whom they do business, seem to think so. Only that business manners are different from social ones.

In social manners, you're not supposed to dwell on money, but there is no doing business without this. Miss Manners would go so far as to say that it would be a violation of business manners not to be frank about cost.

You must not neglect to tell your clients in advance what you charge (including the overtime rate, if you were willing to do overtime, but in this case the fact that you cannot). If they attempt to pay less, you can then remind them of your rate and say pleasantly, "No, I'm afraid you owe me for four hours, because I came here at eight and it is now midnight. That comes to . . ."

This allows them to reply, "Oh, sorry," and rectify the mistake without embarrassment.

Miss Manners hopes that no parent would be so unscrupulous as to question your word about the rate or time, not only for your sake but for the sake of the poor child brought up by such a parent. Should it happen, your reply should be, "I'm sorry you don't trust my word, but in that case, you certainly wouldn't want to trust me with your child." You should not be doing business with dishonest people.

Careless ones, who forgot to watch the time, are another matter—it depends on how careless they are and how often. If you don't want to cease doing business with them, here's a quick way to retrain them:

Have your parents fetch you home at the appointed time, and—because you are certainly not going to neglect your charge, no matter how the parents behave—take the child home with you. Miss Manners promises you (and your parents) that you will only have to do this once.

Coming home to an empty house, and finding a note that says, "My parents insist I be home on time, and I couldn't leave Emma, so I took her home with me," is something they will not care to repeat. Nor will facing your parents when they come to collect the child.

This brings Miss Manners to your hardest question—about avoiding being taken home by the fathers who employ you.

Assuming the worst about people who have done nothing wrong, simply because of the demographic group to which they belong, is as wrong in business as it is socially. Maybe more so.

However, Miss Manners is not willing to insist that you ignore your qualms. Only that you conceal them, in order to avoid insulting your employers. For that she again needs your parents' cooperation.

If they are not able to bring you home (and it would also strengthen the lateness problem if you could say "My mother will be coming for me at midnight"), ask them if you can at least hand them the blame. Doing that, and making it as general as possible—"I'm sorry, but my mother never lets me ride home with men, not even a father, I'm afraid"—at least puts the insult at some distance.

32

KNOW YOUR INNER

by Iyanla Vanzant

Accept your goodness, your beauty, your value, and your worth!

Believe in yourself!

Choose for yourself only those things that are good for you!

Discipline yourself to always do your best and to do it on time!

Excellence, not excess, is the key!

Faith and fearlessness fuel your dreams!

Greatness is the stuff you are made of; act like you know!

Honesty keeps you free of guilt and shame!

Intuition is the teaching from within; pay attention to what you feel!

Joy is what you feel when you love yourself first!

Knowledge is the key to freedom!

Love is what you are, not what you give or get!

Mistakes are lessons that you need to learn!

ABC'S

Never say never! New days bring new ideas and new beginnings!

Order is the law that puts you where you need to be when you need to be there!

Plan prayerfully. Prepare purposefully. Pursue persistently!

Quiet time is necessary for a powerful mind!

Respect yourself and others will do the same!

Self is the most important thing you have to give!

Trust yourself and the process of life!

Unexpected doors are open!

Victory is the prize!

Wisdom is using what you have!

X-pect the best always!

You are the light of the world!

Zealously nurture, honor, and love yourself!

33

IGNORE ADVICE

by Jessica Yu

My first job in film production was noodle wrangler. It was a frozen-pasta commercial, and I was assigned to arrange noodles on plastic forks. For six hours a day.

How did I land in such a glamorous position? A well-meaning acquaintance had assured me that the best way to break into the industry was to work on commercials. But in my three days as a noodle wrangler I learned only two things: (1) rotelle pasta won't stick to a fork, and (2) not all advice is good advice.

Whether you look for it or not, advice will follow you everywhere in life. Some of it is practical: "Don't accept candy/rides/explosives from strangers." Some, dubious: "To overcome a fear of heights, go skydiving." Some, silly: "Sleep facing up and you won't get wrinkles."

Certainty is alluring, especially when you find yourself wailing, "I don't know what I'm doing!" And most advice sounds easy to apply, a one-size-fits-all garment for life. But if you've ever tried on a pair of one-size-fits-all pants, you know how well this approach works. Life requires something a bit more tailored.

After my stint on the pasta commercial, I started working for a company

❝ You can't figure it all out right away. Why don't you give yourself some time? **❞**

161

that made documentaries—films about real life. Many people advised against it: "Documentaries are a dead end"; "No one makes money in those films"; "You're better off going to law/business/bartending school." But the work was exciting, and I was biting into meaty subjects—art, history, politics—and gaining skills: how to do research, how to handle equipment, how to tell a story. I didn't know if I could make a living at it, but I looked forward to it every day.

In 1995, I heard about a writer named Mark O'Brien. He had contracted polio as a child, so severely that he had to live the rest of his life in an iron lung, a machine that helped him breathe. He wrote beautiful poetry about his experiences, and eloquent, powerful essays about the right of disabled people to live independent lives.

I had no funding, but I wanted to make a film about him. Again, the advice rolled in: "Who's going to want to watch a guy in an iron lung? Find a more commercial subject"; "You know, it's not too late to go to law/business/bartending school." I didn't simply plug my ears; some of the advice made sense. But I loved the project, and I knew I'd always regret it if I didn't try.

Besides, what was the worst thing that could happen? Maybe I'd never finish the film, or I'd run out of money and have to go back to noodle wrangling. At least I'd have blundered for a worthwhile cause.

Part of my boldness was inspired by Mark O'Brien himself. If he'd taken his doctors' advice, he'd have been confined to a nursing home. Living on his own, though, he'd gone to college and published several books of poetry and many articles—a lot for any writer, let alone one living with severe disability. But he was the first one to admit that he didn't have all the answers. Mark still struggled every day—not just with polio, but with his work, the world, and the question of how to make a difference. It wasn't the kind of struggle he could win, but as he wrote in one of his poems, "What would we do without the impossible?"

In light of all that, how could I think that making one little film was impossible? It wasn't easy, but it was thoroughly satisfying. Mark's delight, and the pleasure of bringing his life and work to an audience, showed me that ignoring all that "sound" advice was one of the best decisions I ever made.

Of course, you should always listen to *good* advice. And there is such a thing. Early in our relationship, my husband (also named Mark) gave me some of the best advice ever. I was fresh out of college but already feeling stale; six months had passed and I still hadn't figured out what I wanted to do with my life. "I don't know what I'm doing!" I wailed (see above).

"You can't figure it all out right away," Mark said. "Why don't you give yourself some time?"

"How much time?"

"I don't know—ten years?"

"Ten years!" I'd be thirty-one in ten years! "That's an eternity."

"Not compared to the rest of your life."

He was right. None of us want to waste our lives, but we aren't always sure how we want to spend them. And the only way to find out is by wandering a little bit.

So give yourself a chance to get lost, to mess up, to be surprised, to find something meaningful. I guess that's my own little bit of advice—which, of course, you are free to ignore.

ABOUT THE CONTRIBUTORS

CECILE ANDREWS is the author of *The Circle of Simplicity*. She writes a column called "Simplicity" for the *Seattle Times,* and she received her doctorate in education from Stanford University. Her husband writes books about Bill Gates and Microsoft, her daughter is a computer programmer, and her son is an artist in Hawaii. (Everyone is following their passion!)

VANESSA ATLER became the first woman gymnast to go from junior national champion to senior national champion in one year since Dominique Moceanu. In 1996, Atler won her first junior national championship, and she has placed first or second in all three of the senior national championships in which she has competed. Her remarkable ability to combine elegance and power has made her one of the most recognized gymnasts in the world. Vanessa has her own Web site, www.atler.com, which contains additional information about her career.

ILENE "GINGY" BECKERMAN is the author and illustrator of *Love, Loss and What I Wore; What We Do for Love;* and *Mother of the Bride: The Dream, The Reality, The Search for a Perfect Dress*. Her articles have appeared in *Self, Victoria,* and *Ladies' Home Journal* magazines, and in the *New York Times* and the *Los Angeles Times*.

MAGGIE BEHLE began skiing at the age of four and racing when she was eight. When she was fourteen years old, she was named to the U.S. Ski Team and began training for the Nagano Paralympics. She has won two silver medals at the world championships, one bronze medal at the 1997 World Cup, and one World Cup title in the slalom event. She won two bronze medals at the 1998 Paralympics in Nagano, Japan. Most recently, she has decided to attend college to become a writer.

TONYA BOLDEN, a native New Yorker, is the author or editor of more than a dozen books. Among them are *And Not Afraid to Dare: The Stories of Ten African American Women; Strong Men Keep Coming: The Book of African American Men;* and *33 Things Every Girl Should Know*.

COLONEL EILEEN COLLINS graduated in 1979 from U.S. Air Force undergraduate pilot training at Vance Air Force Base, Oklahoma, where she was a T-38 instructor pilot until 1982. She has also been a C-141 aircraft commander and instructor pilot at Travis Air Force Base, California, and an assistant professor of mathematics and a T-41 instructor pilot at the U.S. Air Force Academy in Colorado. She was selected for the astronaut program while attending U.S. Air Force Test Pilot School at Edwards Air Force Base, California, from which she graduated in 1990. Collins became an astronaut in July 1991. A veteran of three space flights, she has logged more than 537 hours in space. She served as pilot on STS-63 (February 2–11, 1995) and STS-84 (May 15–24, 1997) and was the first woman shuttle commander, on STS-93 (July 22–27, 1999).

CASSANDRA DANZ is a member of the New York Horticultural Society and the National Arbor Day Foundation. She is the author of *Mrs. Greenthumbs: How I Turned a Boring Yard into a Glorious Garden and How You Can, Too* (Crown, 1993), which won the Garden Writers Association of America's Quill and Trowel Award, and *Mrs. Greenthumbs Plows Ahead* (Crown, 1998). She's also a contributing editor for *Country Living Gardener* magazine. In 1997, she received the Golden Leaf Award from the Planting Fields Arboretum for her contribution to the advancement of horticulture.

As Mrs. Greenthumbs, she has appeared on many television shows and in two one-woman shows. She began her comedy career at the Second City improvisational theater in Chicago and has appeared in several films and in off-Broadway plays. She is a founding member of the all-female comedy group The High Heeled Women.

BEVERLY DeJULIO is the host of the PBS series *HandyMa'am with Beverly DeJulio* and HGTV's *HomeWise with Beverly DeJulio*. She's a columnist for *Good Housekeeping, Do It Yourself,* and *Arts and Crafts* magazines. She is a radio personality on Chicago's WBBM-AM and author of *HandyMa'am: Home Improvement, Decorating and Maintenance Tips and Projects for You and Your Family.*

NANCY EVANS began her career with editorial positions at *Harper's Weekly* and *Glamour,* then became editor in chief for the Book-of-the-Month Club. She also co-hosted a PBS program on books. Next she was hired as president and publisher of Doubleday Books, and then she started *Family Life* magazine. Most recently, she co-founded iVillage.com: The Women's Network, now the leading online women's network.

SUZANNE FALTER-BARNS is the author of *How Much Joy Can You Stand? A Creative Guide to Facing Your Fears and Making Your Dreams Come True.* She's also the author of a novel, *Doin' the Box Step,* as well as articles and essays in many major publications, including the *New York Times, Self, New Woman, Prevention, Parents,* and *Fitness.* You can read more of her work on her Web site at www.howmuchjoy.com.

NEALE S. GODFREY is an acknowledged expert on family and children's finances. She has been in the financial field for more than twenty years. She began her career as one of the first female executives at Chase Manhattan Bank, in 1972. She then became president of The First Women's Bank and founder of The First Children's Bank. She formed her own company, Children's Financial Network, whose mission is to educate children (and their parents) about money. She is the author of thirteen books, all dealing with money, life-skill, and value issues. Her first book for adults, *Money Doesn't Grow on Trees: A Parent's Guide to Raising Financially Responsible Children,* hit number one on the *New York Times* best-sellers list. She has also developed the first money curriculum for children, for those in grades K–8, as well as a CD-ROM. She is a professional speaker and appears often on such television shows as the *Oprah Winfrey Show,* the *Sally Jessy Raphael Show, Good Morning America,* and *Today,* as well as the television networks CNBC, CNN, and CNNfn.

TINA HOWE is obviously not a cook, but a playwright. Her works include *Painting Churches, Coastal Disturbances,* and *Pride's Crossing.*

LORRAINE JOHNSON-COLEMAN is a master storyteller, a regular commentator on National Public Radio's *Morning Edition,* and author of the best selling *Just Plain Folks.* Lorraine is the winner of a 1998 *Publishers Weekly* Listen Up Award for her *Just Plain Folks* audio book and a 1999 Crystal Jade Award for Excellence for the *Just Plain Folks* radio series. She performed her own original stories for both of these projects.

KENNEDY was raised in suburban bliss just on the outskirts of Portland, Oregon. After graduating from high school in 1990, she packed her '72 VW Bug and headed for Los Angeles, where she became a DJ at the KROQ radio station at the age of nineteen. Two years later she moved to New York and got a gig at MTV, hosting the nightly video show *Alternative Nation.* In addition, Kennedy was a CBS commentator during the 1998 Winter Olympics in Nagano, Japan, and she appears frequently as a speaker at colleges and universities. She is the author of *Hey Ladies! Tales & Tips for Curious Girls.*

LAURA LIPPMAN is a reporter at the *Baltimore Sun* and the author of an award-winning series of detective novels featuring Tess Monaghan, a private detective who loves to eat. Her latest novel is *The Sugar House,* and she is at work on her sixth book in the series. She lives in Baltimore with her husband and springer spaniel.

LOIS LOWRY is the author of many books for young people, including the Newbery Medal winners *Number the Stars* and *The Giver.* She lives in Cambridge, Massachusetts, and Sanbornton, New Hampshire. Both of her houses are filled with memories and secrets.

JUDITH MARTIN'S "Miss Manners" column is read in over two hundred newspapers in the United States and other countries. She's written about the way Americans behave—

or don't behave—since 1978, and most recently she has begun writing "Miss Manners" columns for the Microsoft Network and *eCompany Now* magazine. For many years people thought etiquette was old-fashioned, forgetting that it helps people get along with each other. But after looking around at some of the unfortunate things that happen if manners aren't a part of our lives, Americans got fed up—and said it was time for us to think about courtesy again. In her columns and books, Mrs. Martin tells how etiquette is part of almost everything we do. She's also a novelist and journalist and, as the nation's leading civility expert, can often be seen on TV or heard on the radio. She was a reporter and theater critic at the *Washington Post* before she became Miss Manners full time. Mrs. Martin's most recent book is *Miss Manners' Guide to Domestic Tranquility: The Authoritative Manual for Every Civilized Household However Harried*. She's also written several other Miss Manners books and two novels.

NORMA FOX MAZER has published a total of twenty-nine books, including two collections of short stories, a novelization of a movie, three novels on which she collaborated with her husband, Harry Mazer, and a poetry anthology she co-edited, plus numerous articles and short stories, which have been printed in magazines ranging from *Redbook* to *Child Life* to *English Journal*. She has received a Newbery Honor, the Edgar Allan Poe Award, the Christopher Award, the Lewis Carroll Shelf Award twice, and the Iowa Teen Award twice, and she has been nominated for the National Book Award. Her books have been translated into various languages, including German, French, Spanish, Dutch, Danish, Swedish, Norwegian, and Japanese.

SARA MOULTON, who joined *Gourmet* as a food editor in 1984 and was appointed executive chef in 1987, began her culinary education at the Culinary Institute of America, graduating with highest honors in 1977. She immediately plunged into restaurant work, which consumed her for the next seven years. In 1979, while engaged as the chef of Cybele's Restaurant in Boston, Sara met and started working with Julia Child as the associate chef on the PBS series *Julia Child and More Company*. Shortly thereafter, at Julia's suggestion, Sara capped off her initiation into the culinary arts with a brief but intense apprenticeship to a master chef in Chartres, France. After moving to New York, in 1981, Sara continued her restaurant work as *sous chef* at the Cafe New Amsterdam and *chef tournant* at La Tulipe. In a bid to create an "old girls' network" for women food professionals, she co-founded the New York Women's Culinary Alliance in 1982. A year later she commenced work as an instructor at Peter Kump's New York Cooking School. In 1987, Sara became the executive chef of ABC-TV's *Good Morning America,* working behind the scenes with the show's guest chefs, including such legends as Jacques Pepin, Wolfgang Puck, and Marcella Hazan. She began making on-air appearances a few years ago, and was recently brought into the *GMA* family as food editor. These days, after putting in her hours at *Gourmet,* Sara hosts two daily shows on the Food Network, Cooking Live and *Cooking Live Primetime.*

NAOMI SHIHAB NYE lives in San Antonio, Texas. Some of her recent books are *Habibi* (a novel for teens), *Fuel* (poems), *What Have You Lost?* (an anthology of poems), and *Never in a Hurry* (essays). "Voices" appeared in *Red Suitcase,* a collection of poems published by BOA Editions, Ltd., in 1994.

CAROL M. PERRY, S.U., is currently resident Bible scholar at the Marble Collegiate Church in New York City.

HILARY PRICE, at twenty-five, became the youngest woman ever to have a syndicated daily comic strip. *Rhymes with Orange* appears in newspapers around the country. She has also published a collection of her strips in a book, coincidentally also called *Rhymes with Orange.* A graduate of Stanford University, she began her cartooning career in San Francisco. Her work has appeared in *People, Forbes,* and *Glamour* magazines, as well as in newspapers nationwide. After ten years in the San Francisco Bay Area, she has recently returned to her home state of Massachusetts. *Rhymes with Orange* is now in its fourth year. She has a Web site at www.rhymeswithorange.com.

CHERYL RICHARDSON is the author of *Take Time for Your Life: A Personal Coach's Seven-Step Program for Creating the Life You Want.* Her work as a "life coach" has been covered widely in the media, including *CBS This Morning,* the *New York Times, Self, New Age,* the *Los Angeles Times,* and the *Boston Globe Magazine.* Her free online newsletter, "The Life Makeover Series" (www.cherylrichardson.com), is dedicated to helping people improve the quality of their lives by providing practical, no-nonsense advice to thousands of readers each week. She and her niece Liamarie Johnson live in Massachusetts.

LAURA SCHER leads a life based on the values she wrote about in her essay. She is co-founder, chair, and CEO of Working Assets, a long-distance, credit-card, and online services company that donates a portion of its revenue to nonprofit groups working for peace, human rights, equality, education, and the environment. Working Assets has donated more than $20 million to nonprofit groups since the company was created in 1985.

PATRICIA SCHROEDER is president and chief executive officer of the Association of American Publishers (AAP), the national trade organization of the U.S. book publishing industry. Mrs. Schroeder left Congress undefeated in 1996 after serving in the House of Representatives for twenty-four years. She is currently leading New Century/New

Solutions, a think tank for the Institute for Civil Society in Newton, Massachusetts. Mrs. Schroeder is the author of two books: *Champion of the Great American Family* (Random House, 1989) and *24 Years of House Work . . . and the Place Is Still a Mess* (Andrews McMeel, 1998).

BARBARA SEAMAN is the proud grandmother of Sophia (9), Idalia (6), and Liam (3). She is the author of four books on women's health and also writes biographies and profiles of women. She is a co-founder of National Women's Health Network and a contributing editor of *Ms. Magazine*. She lives in New York City. On March 13, 2000, she was one of twenty activists honored at the dedication of the United States Postal Service's Women's Rights Movement stamp.

SARA SHANDLER is author of the *New York Times* best-seller *Ophelia Speaks: Adolescent Girls Write About Their Search for Self. Ophelia Speaks* has sold over two hundred thousand copies and been published in six languages. Sara was raised in Amherst, Massachusetts, and is now an American studies major at Wesleyan University in Middletown, Connecticut.

KATHLEEN KENNEDY TOWNSEND has been the lieutenant governor of Maryland since 1995. Her core mission is to make Maryland's communities safer, stronger, and more prosperous with innovative, effective solutions to the state's most critical challenges. Before becoming lieutenant governor, Mrs. Townsend served as deputy assistant attorney general in the U.S. Department of Justice; founded and served as executive director of the Maryland Student Service Alliance and made Maryland the first state to include a high-school community service requirement; chaired the Robert F. Kennedy Memorial Foundation and founded the Robert F. Kennedy Human Rights Award; and taught at the University of Pennsylvania, the University of Maryland–Baltimore County, and Essex and Dundalk community colleges. She also serves on the board of the John F. Kennedy Library Foundation.

The eldest child of Robert and Ethel Kennedy, Lieutenant Governor Townsend lives in Baltimore County with her husband, David, a professor at St. John's College in Annapolis. They have four daughters, Meaghan (twenty-two), Maeve (twenty), Kate (sixteen), and Kerry (eight).

LUCILLE TREGANOWAN opened her first auto repair shop, Transmissions by Lucille, in 1973 and now operates two shops in Pittsburgh, employing nearly thirty people. Her weekly half-hour television show, *Lucille's Car Care Clinic,* is broadcast nationally. She is the author of *Lucille's Car Care: Everything You Need to Know from Under the Hood— by America's Most Trusted Mechanic.*

IYANLA VANZANT is the award-winning and best-selling author of *Acts of Faith; The Value in the Valley; Faith in the Valley; One Day My Soul Just Opened Up; In the Meantime; Yesterday, I Cried;* and *Don't Give It Away!* As an empowerment specialist, she lectures and facilitates workshops nationally with a mission to assist in the empowerment of women and men everywhere.

BARBARA WALLRAFF is the author of the best-selling book *Word Court* and writes the "Word Court" column in the *Atlantic Monthly,* resolving readers' disputes about language. She is also a senior editor of the *Atlantic.* Since 1983 she has reviewed the galleys of every article and story scheduled to appear in that magazine, advising authors about tone, style, consistency, and grammar.

CHELY WRIGHT wanted to be a country singer since she was three years old. She came from a musical family and by age eleven was singing professionally in Kansas City, her hometown. In her teens she formed her own band, County Line. As a junior in high school, she performed at the Ozark Jubilee in Missouri. At age eighteen she earned cast membership in the "Country Music U.S.A." show at the Opryland theme park in Nashville. Armed with her arsenal of country music knowledge, Chely began recording in 1994. She won the Top New Female Vocalist award at the 1995 Academy of Country Music Awards. In 1997, "Shut Up and Drive" became her first top-ten hit and the centerpiece for her debut collection on MCA, *Let Me In.*

JESSICA YU is a filmmaker based in Los Angeles. Her films include the Academy Award–winning documentary *Breathing Lessons: The Life and Work of Mark O'Brien* and *The Living Museum* (HBO), a portrait of an art community in a New York psychiatric institution, as well as several short films and television projects. Her work has been broadcast and exhibited in festivals around the world.

ABOUT THE EDITOR

SUZANNE HARPER is the editor-in-chief of *Disney Adventures* magazine. She is the author of three children's books: *Boitano's Edge: Inside the Real World of Figure Skating; Clouds;* and *Lightning.* She lives in New York City.

ACKNOWLEDGMENTS

We gratefully acknowledge the following for permission to use their work in this book.

Cecile Andrews for "Simplify Your Life." Copyright © 2001 by Cecile Andrews. Used by permission of the author.

Vanessa Atler for "Stay Connected with Your Family." Copyright © 2001 by Vanessa Atler. Used by permission of the author.

Ilene Beckerman for "Remember, Nobody's Perfect." Copyright © 2001 by Ilene Beckerman. Used by permission of the artist.

Maggie Behle for "Act on Your Passion!" Copyright © 2001 by Maggie Behle. Used by permission of the author.

Tonya Bolden for "Get a Mentor, Be a Mentor." Copyright © 2001 by Tonya Bolden. Used by permission of the author.

Cassandra Danz for "Plant a Garden!" Copyright © 2001 by Cassandra Danz. Used by permission of the author.

Beverly DeJulio for "Get Handy Around the House." Copyright © 2001 by Beverly DeJulio. Used by permission of the author.

Nancy Evans for "Explore All Your Options." Copyright © 2001 by Nancy Evans. Used by permission of the author.

Suzanne Falter-Barns for "Follow Your Dreams—Especially if They're Embarrassing." Copyright © 2001 by Suzanne Falter-Barns. Used by permission of the author.

Neale S. Godfrey for "Learn to Save Money—and Invest It." Copyright © 2001 by Neale S. Godfrey. Used by permission of the author.

Tina Howe for "How to Make an After-Your-Boyfriend-Dumps-You-for-Your-Best-Friend Pineapple Upside-Down Cake." Copyright © 2001 by Tina Howe. Used by permission of the author.

Lorraine Johnson-Coleman for "Honor the Make-Do Mamas in Your Life." Copyright © 2001 by Lorraine Johnson-Coleman. Used by permission of the author.

Kennedy for an excerpt from *Hey Ladies!* by Kennedy. Copyright © 1999 by Lisa Kennedy Montgomery. Used by permission of Doubleday, a division of Random House, Inc.

Laura Lippman for "Listen to Your Body." Copyright © 2001 by Laura Lippman. Used by permission of the author.

Lois Lowry for "Write Your Name on a Wall." Copyright © 2001 by Lois Lowry. Used by permission of the author.

Judith Martin for "How to Mind Your Manners." Copyright © 2001 by Judith Martin. Reprinted by permission.